AND JUST LIKE THAT

Using Life Jolts to Create the Next Best
Version of Yourself in Leadership and Life

Karen Burrows McKnight

First published by Ultimate World Publishing 2021
Copyright © 2021 Karen McKnight

ISBN

Paperback: 978-1-922597-43-4
Ebook: 978-1-922597-44-1

Cover design: Ultimate World Publishing
Layout and typesetting: Ultimate World Publishing
Editor: Isabelle Russell
Cover photo: icemanphotos-Shutterstock.com

Ultimate World Publishing
Diamond Creek,
Victoria Australia 3089
www.writeabook.com.au

Dedication

For Greg, an amazing person, not to mention a supportive and caring husband and father.

For my awesome children, Larissa, Alison and Carter, who are central to who I have become.

For my incredible Family of Origin, with gratitude.

For all those who have walked and talked with me on this complex and enriching life journey—may it continue!

Testimonials

"The successful teacher truly understands the journey of their student. Karen shares her experiences, perspectives and strategies to help shape the reader in their personal journey of self awareness and growth. This straightforward guide simplifies a process that many find daunting. Karen's passion, commitment and love of helping others jumps off the pages. Her curiosity is infectious and lights a fire in all those who are fortunate enough to cross her path. And Just Like That, you find yourself thinking about your thinking—and that is what it is all about."

Rob Vanden Broek
President and CEO
Sierra Supply Chain Services

"*And Just Like That* offers a compassionate and practical approach to respond to life's jolts—big and small, internal and external. The book has a conversational nature and coaching-like rhythm that will resonate and be actionable for a wide range of leaders and people. The approach is informed by Karen's own deeply reflective process for responding to her own life jolts, combined with her extensive experience as a coach working with senior leaders. The result is a lovely invitation for meaningful learning and growth."

Melinda Sinclair, D. Phil, Chartered Business Coach™
Executive Coach, founder of PeopleDynamics Learning
Group. Designer of the ICF accredited Business Coaching
Advantage™ coach training program and the in-depth
FutureWise Leadership program.

Contents

PRELUDE

Why Me, Why This, Why Now?

"You are allowed to be both a masterpiece and a work in progress simultaneously."
Sophia Bush

Before jumping in, I thought it appropriate to first address who I am and how and why I came to undertake this process.

When I think about who I am to write this book, I want to clarify that I am not extraordinary. Like you, I am just trying to do my best to navigate a life that is, for the most part, good. I try to bring my best and be my best in all my roles. They all make up who I am—a wife, a mother, a daughter, a sister, an aunt, a friend, a learner, a colleague, a coach, a leader, a facilitator. Like you, I have experienced my share of life's inevitable ups and downs, and so far, I have survived every one of my worst days.

While I have navigated my own life jolts, and will continue to do so—big and small, positive and negative, internally generated and externally imposed, I don't have a shocking or horrific story to tell. I have experienced joy and sorrow like everyone else, and I acknowledge that these extremes are more intense for some than for others. Whatever level of intensity felt is real for the person experiencing it, and is deserving of time, energy and attention.

> *"I believe that life is amazing. And then it's awful. And then it's amazing again. And in between the amazing and awful it's ordinary and mundane and routine. Breathe in the amazing, hold on through the awful and relax and exhale during the ordinary. That's just living heartbreaking, soul-healing, amazing, awful, ordinary life. And it's breathtakingly beautiful."*
>
> L.R. Knost

I am blessed. I live life, as I always have done, in a deep way. I experience things fully, I feel things profoundly, I learn continuously, I think complexly, I want to know and understand fully, and I care. What I know for sure is that love is big enough to hold it all—and that my capacity for love is immense.

I am grateful for every jolt in my life—each one has allowed me to grow and become a better version of myself and thus be there more fully for myself and others. I do not pretend to have all the answers and I am as perfectly imperfect as anyone... but I do remain open to life—all of it, the full experience. The way I walk on this planet and the lessons I have learned as a result may support others in figuring it out for themselves. That is my hope. This is my offering.

If you know one story you know one story—this is a snapshot of mine. The process I share in this book is intended to be customized to your story.

When the COVID-19 pandemic hit, we were in Florida with several other couples, enjoying some much-needed sunshine, good food, relaxation and conversation with great friends. As the news became more dire, I could barely pull myself away from the stories unfolding on the screen. We were in a beautiful setting, on holiday, yet as each day went by the news seemed to get grimmer and as each shocking revelation occurred the impact of the pandemic started to sink in. Once we received the unprecedented news that school was going to be cancelled and people were going to be ordered to stay home, it really hit.

We scrambled to get flights home and began our 14-day quarantine in our basement. As the days rolled into each other, and changes were occurring in a rapid-fire way, I felt like being physically stuck in my basement was a metaphor for emotionally hitting rock bottom.

Almost overnight, all of the leadership coaching facilitations I had booked for my work throughout 2020 were cancelled. While my one-on-one work with clients continued, and became even more in demand, I felt unprepared and inadequate to support leaders in such complex, uncertain and unprecedented times. I gathered strength and did what I could to stay positive, supportive and strong in service of the incredible challenges people were facing in life and work. I stayed in coaching mode, asking questions and helping my clients create the best possible scenarios given the uncertainty and the immense importance of the decisions they were facing. I tried to read, research and stay connected to the turbo-charged rate of change that was occurring. But inside, I was panicking, and it was taking all my energy just to get through the days. Personally, the pandemic was hitting me on all levels as well as impacting my family and friends. There was an unfolding story within myself, in those close to me and worldwide. Life as we knew it, not just one element but in its entirety, was being impacted by the pandemic. It "jolted us open" and thus, by necessity, we all had and still have to look at things differently. I was aware that I was part of an unprecedented collective grief that I had no resources or prior experience to draw on to make sense of it. I wondered if this was some message from the universe that I had already contributed what I was meant to and maybe it was time to pack it in from a work perspective. And if that wasn't enough, as the year rolled on, I started having heart palpitations. It was as if I was being told to stop, listen and pay attention differently.

This culminated in a very scary day where the heart palpitations were accompanied by a severe pain that lasted all day. I couldn't get off the couch and ended up in the emergency department. Not a fun place to be, all alone, in the middle of a pandemic. This led to a series of tests, ultrasounds and wearing a heart monitor for two weeks before having the virtual consult with the cardiologist to get the results. He began by saying that he would just start with the end to ease my mind. I remember his exact words when he said, "Your heart actually works better than most people's," which made me laugh. I explained that his description was interesting because if he knew me, he would know that "heart" and caring is what I am all about and that is precisely why the last few months had been so difficult for me. It shifted the conversation from a formal doctor-patient interaction to a more personal one that ended with him emphasizing that as hard as it is during the current reality, if I didn't get a handle on my stress, it would become an actual physical heart issue and the two of us would be having a very different kind of conversation.

And Just Like That, something had to change. I am blessed to have trusted people in my life with whom I was able to share what was going on for me and start processing my experience. I joined my niece in signing up for an online course about the psychology of dealing with COVID-19. I began to gather input to create an approach that would increase my chance of navigating life in the midst of chaos and uncertainty at a level I had no experience with. I eventually wrote "Day 1" on my calendar on Monday, October 19, 2020. While I wasn't quite sure what that meant I set the intention that this was the beginning of my evolution into the next best version of myself, in my leadership and my life.

I was no stranger to self-development, and something within me was reminding me of that, but I now knew that I had to go all in. I needed to trust that I knew where to look as I had in the past. As I reviewed my life, I realized that I had been impacted by a series of life jolts which compelled me to think deeply, regroup and respond optimally to achieve success and peace in terms of whatever I was facing. I feel like I was hurled into a life of awareness and growth by some difficult and rebellious teenage years, trying to figure out who I was. Then, the enjoyment of rebalancing during my university, marriage and early career years—fulfilling a lifelong dream of becoming a teacher. Next came the painful years of infertility followed by the joy of becoming a parent through adopting three incredible kids. Those amazingly positive jolts propelled me to a whole other level and understanding of who I was meant to be as a mom and who I have become as a person. And then there were the jolts and ensuing growth from career change, working on my Master's degree while raising small kids and then being knocked off balance again when the kids left home in rapid succession. A jolt of such mixed emotions and one that, although as a parent one works toward for years, I felt sorely unprepared for. This sent me into a tailspin and yet another round of "Who am I? And what is the world calling me to do?" Again, I was caught seemingly unaware in spite of having committed most of my adult life to being actively engaged in personal development. And now a global pandemic—really?

I became curious and wanted to know how to make sense of it all. As I reviewed how I navigated things in my life, I realized that at each one of the turning points, the pivot points jolted me, but they jolted me towards an intense period of learning, growing and researching the particular themes around the situation. Eventually, by having the courage to stay in the process something new emerged and I entered the next phase of development, awareness and another, better iteration of myself. The joy and pain, the whole spectrum of experience and the subsequent learning and action, while not necessarily easy during the process, enabled release from the confinement of the metaphorical basement every time.

Day 1 for me was the beginning of the next phase of research in my own life. I needed to start paying attention differently to my internal world, so I could become better able to meet the external world. I was inspired to experiment and create the next best version of myself, career and contribution-wise, as well as becoming a better human being in all the roles I am blessed with. I started a morning routine devoted to the inner thinking and exploration I knew I needed to do in order to figure it out.

I committed to wellness, healthier eating, gaining insight, learning and remaining curious and open. As each morning passed, I began to notice a shift. I realized I was showing up differently at work and in my personal relationships and life. I realized I was infusing all that I was learning and thinking about into every aspect of these uncertain times. Just as I had been encouraging others to pivot in their leadership and life I started to gain evidence of its power as I saw hints of progress in my own process.

Day 1 symbolized a new beginning—the first step in the creation of a virtuous cycle of health, wellness and my next level of contribution. I felt re-energized in all ways; my sleep improved and my intellectual curiosity peaked. I began gaining the confidence to work virtually, connect creatively and contribute to others even if I couldn't meet with them in person.

When we pay attention to our internal world, we equip ourselves to be better able to meet the external world—in all its complexity. The emerging evidence was proving that I could meet whatever was before me just as I had done every other time I'd been faced with a challenge. After each issue was met effectively, I felt empowered, stronger and even more ready to face life with hope, positivity and inspiration… and thus more able to contribute fully, to give back. It is an inside-out experience.

My invitation is to be open when you read this book, focus on what resonates for you. Not all of it will—that's the point—it is your process, your content and it is unique and specific to you. You get to decide what's next. You are on your own path of creating the next best version of yourself. I have given you the background of how I came to write this book. Over the past 20 years I have been privileged to coach senior executives, to facilitate and consult in organizations and to lead CEO learning groups. I also have a teaching background and my decades of living and learning and the whole spectrum of ups and down that go along with the challenges I have successfully navigated. All of the above informs what I share with you throughout the following pages.

This isn't a quick fix; it is a process that proposes questions for you to step into should you choose to really take up the invitation. I don't pretend to have the ultimate answer for you—I certainly haven't even figured out all the answers for myself and I realize that I never will. Creating the best version of yourself is a process, a journey, a pilgrimage, if you will.

My hope is that I provide not only interesting insights that may resonate, but also the kind of input and ideas that will spur your thinking and, most importantly, give you the inspiration to take action in your own life. This includes thinking about things in new ways, remaining open to considering different perspectives, cultivating hope through a process that you can believe in, and experimenting with new behaviours. This is also about embracing these things and making them authentically your own to create and evolve into the next level of your best self, whatever that may be for you in your leadership and life.

INTRODUCTION

Stepping Into Life's Equations

While the concept of becoming the next best version of yourself sounds simple, it can be a struggle.

Life can be compared to a math equation, and in any equation there are a number of key steps:

- First, there needs to be an understanding of what the variables are. This requires critical thinking and the ability to acknowledge the range and specifics of the variables on the table. Life jolts shift our priorities and thus change the variables at play. We need to be aware of each of the components we are facing.

- Once the variables are identified, there is a process to determine how the variables go together to create the question. This, too, requires critical thinking, as well as openness and curiosity with respect to the potential connections between the variables. Looking at how the variables can and do work together is essential.

- After the question is formed, next comes the process of solving the equation. This takes time, experimentation, thinking outside the box, intention, work and correcting missteps, being informed not only by the parts along the way that fit but also by the mistakes in service of resolution.

- Once the equation has been solved, we get to live for a while in that solved equation. This is more than achieving the goal or new level or checking it off your to-do list, it is also about the feeling state you achieve when you solve it. These are the times in life when all is well—it has been figured out, for now.

- Next, a variable changes. Sometimes we don't see it coming, sometimes we plan for it. A variable change can also evolve over time. It takes being present, aware and sometimes requires us to muster up the courage to recognize and accept that one or more variables have changed. Sometimes, the jolt comes unexpectedly, even harshly, and stops us in our tracks—we know and feel the shift immediately! Regardless of the size or approach, change is in front of us and we must confront it.

- Finally, the cycle repeats. We return to analyzing the new set of variables, their complexities, how the elements are connected to the new variables and the implications of the interactions between all facets.

This is an ongoing process in life—we are always actively engaged in our own life equation. In order to live more often in the "solved equation", we can benefit from an approach to support us. And Just Like That, a suggested process follows.

The purpose of this book is not only to offer insights that resonate with you, but also to provide the kind of input and thinking that will inspire you to think differently and take action. The invitation is to bring the ideas to life in your own circumstances.

This book is divided into three sections followed by an afterword, broken down as follows:

- Section A—**The Foundations**—what the development work is based on:
  - Pay Attention
  - Connect With Your Best
  - Befriend Imperfection
  - Choose Your Mindset

- Section B—**And Just Like That**—understanding and embracing what you are facing and cultivating the conditions for the ultimate And Just Like That to emerge:
  - Embrace The Jolts
  - Take On The Transition

- Section C—**The Process**—customizing a process to use the jolt to create the next, best version of yourself in leadership and life:
  - Cultivate Relationships
  - Seek and Gather Input
  - Experiment
  - Reflect
  - The Aha—the second And Just Like That

Each chapter offers "teach pieces" around the themes and then has three applications:

- **Connect It**—connecting the concepts to work and life examples
- **Apply It**—exercises to customize the concept to your current reality
- **Commit To It**—questions to guide you to increase the chance of success in meeting your goals. The call to action for each chapter is "will you, or won't you?"

You can decide how much time to allocate to the application of the ideas in your own life and work. You may want to either actually or metaphorically open a file to record your thoughts as you go through this book. What works for you? How do you like to process and record this type of thinking and work? Who, if anyone, might support you and even provide "check-ins" and accountability or does it work best for it to be a solo journey?

- Are you a notetaker?
  - Computer document?
  - Notes on mobile phone?
  - A journal or notebook?
  - Loose paper?
  - Post-it notes?
- Do you prefer to speak it?
  - Voice-to-text on Microsoft Word?
  - Recordings on your phone?
- A combination of some or all of these?
- Some other way?

In this book I invite you to take the next step toward the ideal given your current circumstances while being present to "what is" and radically accepting it. It is about developing and expanding your capabilities to navigate the jolts. The important thing is to start your own process by making it real. And Just Like That, you have started the journey to take your leadership and life to the next level of growth to achieve greater ease, happiness and alignment.

SECTION A

The Foundations

*"Regardless of the vision a structure's height is
determined by the depth and strength of the foundation."*
Karen Burrows McKnight

There is a foundation to work from and build on when it comes
to personal and leadership development. This is more than an
intellectual exercise. It is a human experience and a practice.
Awareness is the first step—we can't change anything we are
not aware of. We also need to know what our ideal is—who we
are at our best as people and leaders. Additionally, we have to
embrace our imperfections and cultivate a healthy relationship
with our "cracks". Finally, we need to be aware of and choose
our mindset as it isn't just what we see, but how we see it, that
defines our experience.

We can be leaders in our lives and at work if we have the intention
and courage to step onto and follow the path of development.
Understanding and internalizing these foundations creates the
conditions for the work to be done. What follows in the first section
are the four foundational pieces for this kind of developmental
work:

- Awareness—Pay Attention
- Best Self—Connect with Your Best
- The Cracks—Befriend Imperfection
- Approach—Choose Your Mindset

CHAPTER 1

Pay Attention

"What we achieve and who we become are directly related to what we pay attention to."
Karen Burrows McKnight

"Not everything that can be faced can be changed but nothing can be changed until it is faced."
James Balvin

You were likely drawn to this book because you are curious. You are motivated and ready to look at ways to move to the next level of your best self—in leadership and in life. The starting place is paying attention. The truth is that you can't change or respond to anything you aren't aware of. You don't know what you don't know. Once you start paying attention differently everything changes and things become possible in a new way.

Life is full of commitments, distractions and responsibilities. Our lives and work are consumed by getting things done: leading our organizations, striving for success in our various roles, raising our kids, engaging in our passions and contributing to our communities.

The momentum of life absorbs us. We become comfortable in our patterns, rhythms, habits and frenetically working through our never-ending to-do lists. We are likely accomplishing many things, at times even extremely well. But are we really paying attention? And what are we paying attention to? Paying attention gives us the benefit of pausing and wondering if and how the elements in our life are serving us.

The harsh reality is that life jolts are inevitable. Response is required when the variables shift—however that happens. We have to adjust and pivot. Change is one of the only certainties in life other than the fact that none of us will live forever. The question is: do you want to let life happen *to* you or do you want to navigate it in a way that works best *for* you?

If you don't embrace this reality and begin paying attention differently and intentionally, you are destined to be in reaction mode and you will have less chance of achieving your optimal life. You will be susceptible to a victim mentality and all the connected stressors that this triggers. You will not be able to effectively plan because you won't be clear about what's even happening let alone be able to do anything about it. You will get caught up in presumptions and make mistakes or missteps that may not align with what serves you or what you actually want out of life.

Awareness is about understanding from multiple perspectives— intellectual, feeling and meaning. It is about witnessing yourself, others and your circumstances. It is about paying attention to how an interaction, a circumstance, an element of reality is unfolding and the connected impact on everything related to it. It is about activating your radar with all your senses in an attempt to expand your capacity to hold complexity and polarities in the palm of one hand. It is an intention, an approach. It is about noticing, questioning, being curious. Intentional awareness is about not buying into how you are understanding something but rather delving into all the ways you might understand it. It is about getting to the heart of the matter. It is about making the decision to analyze and think about self, others and life in a deeper way, a broader way, and in a way that seeks to know, and truly connect with the feelings, the situation, the reality and the desired results in a more comprehensive, complete way.

Life jolts force us to pay attention in a new way. Let's use them in service of our growth and development instead of toward our demise.

There are two elements of awareness—internal and external— which exist on three levels:

- Awareness of self
- Awareness of others
- Awareness of the current reality

Internal awareness relates to how we pay attention to ourselves— our ability to monitor our inner world.

How clearly and realistically do you see yourself? What is your ability to recognize *what is* with respect to your:

• values	• passions	• interests
• responsibilities	• relationships	• goals
• triumphs	• disappointments	• alignment with life
• strengths	• gifts	• experiences
• weaknesses	• emotions	• behaviour
• beliefs	• truths	• motivations

External awareness is about how others view us in terms of the same factors. It is important, and often very helpful, to be open to the perspectives of others. We have our intentions about how we want to show up, but the question is—do our intentions align with our impact on others? We don't necessarily need to agree with someone else's perspective, but we benefit from being open to seeing and hearing what they are saying to deepen our understanding of ourselves. We can be big enough to hold multiple perspectives without buying into the parts that aren't true for us. We can use this information and input in service of our own well-being and betterment if we are open to it.

In addition to awareness of how we are perceived by others, there is also an important element of external awareness in how we view, relate to and understand to others. It is in this reciprocal process that we are able to have compassion and understanding for ourselves and others. Relationships hold up mirrors and we benefit from that awareness if we are open to really taking in what we see and learning from the dynamic of the interaction between ourselves and others.

From an external awareness perspective, we also need to be acutely aware of the particulars of our current reality. We need to pay attention to all the factors and perspectives and be open to what is true for ourselves, others and our environment. Consider the following:

- What is the situation trying to tell you?
- What are the multiple perspectives or truths?
- Where are the elements of control?

Listen with all your senses, resources, skills, preferences and gifts. Resist dismissing what doesn't resonate or what you don't agree with. Acknowledge the "shoulds" that your mind is telling you to follow.

Awareness empowers us—but how do we become more aware? It has to be cultivated. Things like control, power, ego and status can get in the way of people accurately assessing self, others and situations. Ego has to be put aside for true awareness. As Robin Sharma says, "A bad day for the ego is a good day for the soul." True awareness has to be collected in non-biased, objective ways and can lead to powerful paradigm shifts.

When you pay attention more acutely, you become aware of how you experience something, particularly when you are interacting with or responding to stressful situations. Where do you feel it and how does it manifest itself—flushed cheeks, perspiration, stomach pangs, heart palpitations, energy surge? How do you cue yourself to pause, be present, scan the current reality and ask yourself, firstly, "Am I taking this in?", and if so, "How am I taking this in?"

As we become more aware, we benefit—even if the process of gaining greater awareness feels hard. We gain new information, understanding, knowledge, confidence, patience and clarity because we are more attuned to what is. We shine light on the components of greater happiness, peace and ease with the world. We also become empowered and more able to cultivate satisfying relationships by having the courage to put ego aside and engage in a realistic, humble, honest, vulnerable assessment of our reality. We can access and feel more connected to what balance looks and feels like for us, as individuals and in the context of our particular and unique circumstances.

It is awareness that enables us to know what centre is—our true north.

> *"Morihei Ueshiba, the founder of the martial art of Aikido, was a small man who could turn back the onslaughts of opponents many times his weight and size with movements that were imperceptible. He appeared to be perfectly centred, anchored to the ground in an extraordinary way. But this was not the case. His ability came not from superior balance, but from superb levels of self-awareness. As he described it, he was quicker to notice when he was off balance and faster at returning to centre.*
>
> *He perfectly describes how to move in harmony with life rather than to resist it. First, we must know what "centre" feels like. We must know who we are, our patterns of behaviour, our values, our intentions. The ground of our identity and experience must feel familiar to us; we must know what it feels like to be standing in it. But we don't expect that we will be perfectly balanced in that centre all the time. We know that we will drift into the wrong activities or be thrown off balance by life's chaos. But we will also recognize when we're moved off too far and will be able to recall ourselves more quickly to who we want to be."*
>
> Margaret Wheatley,
> Leadership and the New Science

CONNECT IT

Taking a true leadership role in our lives and work begins with paying attention, which leads to awareness. If you think about the leaders and people you most admire and are inspired to follow, how would you rate their level of awareness? Of self? Of others? Of the world? How would you rate yourself?

A senior level client I know was reporting to a newly appointed CEO. They have a relationship based on mutual respect that was cultivated over years of working as peers, and my client began reporting to him given the colleague's promotion to CEO. There was a new line of business being developed and launched that my client was leading with her team. They were creative, collaborative and successful in completing the project in spite of challenging market conditions. The launch was not without its glitches, but the resounding success could be measured in feedback from new and existing customers, record sales and profits in addition to high profile media coverage about the innovation and effectiveness of the product as a solution for consumers.

The CEO's feedback to the project leader and the team did not appear to align with the impressive reality. In his post-launch address to the team the CEO acknowledged all the wins, yet spent the majority of his comments focused on the challenges at the various phases of the process. The team left feeling deflated, unmotivated and even confused.

Because my client had a good relationship with the CEO, she had the courage to initiate a conversation to uncover what was behind the seemingly negative focus. She said she was curious about the comments to the group and shared the impact of the feedback on the team's motivation. The CEO was shocked and had no idea that his comments would have landed in that way. What became clear was that the CEO was actually feeling quite insecure about his ability to fulfill his new role effectively. He believed that his job required him to "know more" and share his knowledge to ensure missteps would be avoided moving forward. He was not conscious that his message or delivery would be received in the way it was. His intention was to add value and appear to be a competent and strong leader. It ended up not really being about the team's competency at all but more about a lack of awareness of how the CEO's own insecurity impacted upon his approach and coloured the feedback he gave to the team. He had been following a playbook in his mind that a good CEO is able to help a team course correct for future endeavours. While that is certainly part of the role, it is vital to have an awareness of the relative weight of all factors in a given situation and be sure to focus attention appropriately. My client's ability to have an honest conversation, without judging or igniting defensiveness, enabled a new level of awareness that shifted how the CEO saw himself, his role and how he planned future communication with the team. Awareness can empower leaders to better align their intentions and actions.

In our personal lives we can also get caught up in our version of the "right" way to be or the "shoulds" connected to our roles. A parent may be excited to try a new parenting method as outlined in the latest bestselling manual, enthused by chatter about how brilliantly it works for others. Yet they are frustrated by repeated attempts to implement the strategy when it clearly isn't working for their child. A parent's realistic awareness of themselves and how their child experiences the things they try can increase the chance of positive results. Again, the intention can be honourable but without an honest assessment of how the strategy lands (or not) for the individual child, it is an exercise in frustration and impedes the goal.

We can also come across in ways we don't intend if we aren't aware of message, tone and manner. Think about a time where someone has questioned your angry sounding response, to which you reply, "I am not upset and didn't mean to come across that way at all!" Upon reflection, you realize that your worry over not getting the work deadline finished before dinner must have affected how your words came out without realizing it.

APPLY IT

So how can we gain increased awareness? Here are a couple of things to try.

Life Categories Exercise

The following exercise helps raise awareness in all areas of our lives.

Thinking about these various categories can help identify where you are and where you wish to go. Consider the following:

Livelihood/Career—job, role in terms of how you support your lifestyle

Personal Development—enhancing and supporting your learning, growth, skills

Finances—budgeting, saving, education funds, estate planning, retirement goals

Health & Wellness—physical health, exercise, nutrition and emotional well-being

Fun—the "just for fun" stuff, including sports, games and music

Social Life—the activities, events, get-togethers, destinations, venues, clubs

Family—kids, spouse, extended family, family of origin

Home—the physical environment you call home, not just the place but how is it curated to be called "home" and also other environments (including nature) where you feel at home

Creativity—how is your creativity being expressed, including through art, music, writing or other creative expression

Relationships—intimate, friends, family, colleagues, mentors, peers, acquaintances

You can gain different kinds of awareness by using these categories in a number of ways. Try asking different questions such as:

- What is currently present in each category for you?
- What do you notice?
- How satisfied are you with the quality and nature of your content in each area?
- What would ideal look like?

- How does the current reality feel for you in each area?
- Where are the gaps in terms of reality and ideal?
- What is possible?

Experimenting with the wheel format below can be helpful. What are the key components presently in each area? If the centre is zero and the outside of the circle is ten, create some metrics around the contents of your categories. When complete, take a step back and look. Where would you like to focus? Where do you need to focus to assess what is working and what could be even better? In what area or areas does your current challenge lie?

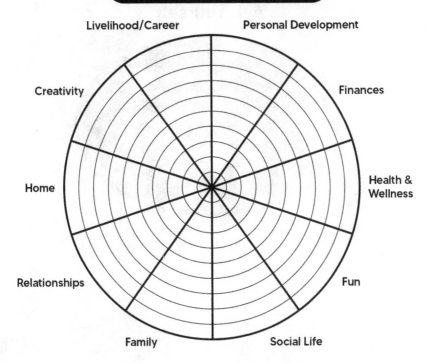

35

Multiple Perspectives Feedback Exercise

In addition to gaining awareness about your life categories, receiving feedback is another important way to guide you in what to pay attention to. There are various kinds of 360-style assessments—many of which are well researched and comprehensive. My experience is that being open to asking for feedback from others to gain awareness is helpful and essential. It doesn't have to be a complicated process. Try this:

Multiple Perspectives Feedback

Ask Yourself

- What do you notice about yourself when you are at your best?

- What do you notice about yourself when you are not at your best?

Then Ask Others

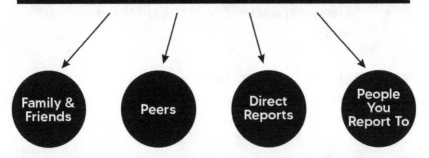

- • What do you notice about me when I'm at my best?
- • What do you notice about me when I'm not at my best?

Family & Friends — Peers — Direct Reports — People You Report To

Ask people you align with and challenge yourself to also ask people you do not to gain full perspective

When you ask these questions, the purpose is to make note of and take in what people say without responding to or defending what you hear. The most effective way to gain honest feedback is to ask for 15 minutes of someone's time to have a conversation without giving them the questions ahead of time. Explain that you are actively engaged in a learning process and you would like their perspective on a couple of things. During the conversation, pose the questions and listen to what they have to say. It is powerful and can be transformative. The key is to avoid getting bogged down by the details or derailed by the feedback, particularly from the second question. Simply take it in. Once you have gathered the information focus on the top five areas people highlighted about you when you are at your best and the top three themes people noticed about you when you are not at your best.

- What rises to the top?
- What are the themes?
- What resonates?
- What can you learn?
- How does it inform you?
- Where do you want and need to focus to move toward an ideal state?

Use what you learned to increase the amount of time you spend "at your best" and find ways to notice and redirect when you are triggered and not able to show up optimally.

As mentioned at the outset of this chapter, life and work are busy. Things are urgent, things happen quickly and require us to be on the treadmill of life. You may be thinking that there is no time for paying attention in this way. You may also face resistance and believe that you have been successful in your habits and ways of interacting with life and career—so why prioritize this kind of work? You have always figured out solutions and that is why you have achieved the level of success you have enjoyed to date. You may feel that you are adept at being aware of who you are, how you show up and what you need to do. That may be true, but what else could be possible? Even if you come up with the same answer or response after additional information and reflection, you will now know for sure it is right for you and for this situation. Thus, you can commit fully. What might be possible if you expanded your awareness and resisted buying into the response patterns you are used to? What if awareness leads you to better, more aligned and satisfying outcomes in terms of thought, feelings, actions and results?

COMMIT TO IT

PAY ATTENTION

- How can you pay attention differently?
- What are you more aware of now – in your life and about yourself?
- How do these realizations relate to your current situation?
- Where are the gaps between your current reality and what would be better?

Will you or won't you take action in terms of how you pay attention?

CHAPTER 2

Connect with Your Best

"Wherever you go there you are."
Jon Kabat-Zinn

"Make the most of yourself, for that is all there is of you."
Ralph Waldo Emerson

We have to know what "at our best" feels and looks like in order to "be there" more often. This is especially true when facing life challenges. Knowing the state of being that for you is optimal supports the process of replicating it. You are unique and it is your specific qualities, characteristics, gifts, skills, personality traits, knowledge, wisdom, callings and presence that, when activated fully, create the experience of being in flow with life.

It is easy to lose track of who we are at our best, especially when going through a challenging or an exciting time. We often get preoccupied and consumed by the chaos of the unknown or we become immersed in the energy of what is new. There is panic in realizing that we aren't in the solved equation anymore and thus it is even harder to adequately meet the challenge in a way that serves us and the situation. It is vital to pause and connect with those qualities of excellence that still exist within us even if they feel inaccessible in the moment. How can those ways of being come alive in the present?

People often live in "shoulds" which may not be connected to who they are at their best. It is easy to buy into a version of how you should be acting or thinking when facing a life jolt versus what feels right for you and how you can be most effective in meeting the situation.

If you can't access and thus show up at your best, it will be difficult to navigate the challenge in a way that will work for you. You will get caught up in an adrenaline-fuelled reactive state. You will be blocked from making decisions in terms of thinking, feeling and acting in ways that are effective. When jolts become all-consuming, your best self can become inaccessible. Circumstances can block access because you are in reactive mode. It is easy to be so focused on the immediate things that need to be attended to, decided on, acted on, that you accept, either consciously or unconsciously, that this is just who I am right now—even if it isn't ideal. The circumstances or jolt seem to define who you are, create a swirl of action and momentum and there can be a sense that you are not at choice. Practice being intentional to avoid this type of spiral. Again, it all starts with paying attention to raise awareness so you can make more effective choices.

Awareness is the critical starting point, then connecting to who you are at your best and how that feels starts to build the next step. You have to know what best feels like to cultivate more of it. This creates the ability to be "in response to" whatever you are facing or initiating. Positive psychology informs this process.

We all want to live happier, more engaged and meaningful lives. Positive psychology impactfully contributes to our understanding of how to achieve this. After years of addressing and fixing what is "wrong" from a mainstream psychology perspective, positive psychology emerged to focus and build on the best of the human condition. Spearheaded by Martin Seligman and Mihaly Csikszentmihalyi, positive psychology highlights and explores what makes life worthwhile, productive and fulfilling, in all its complexity. Positive psychology provides new evidence to help us better understand why and how people flourish.

Seligman describes positive psychology as the "scientific study of optimal human functioning that aims to discover and promote the factors that allow individuals and communities to thrive." The three pillars, positive experiences, positive traits and positive institutions capitalize on who we are at our best and our ability to connect to the five elements of the science; positive emotions, engagement, relationships, meaning and achievement.

Cultivating positive emotions and identifying and expanding on strengths supports us in accessing and becoming who we are at our best. When we use our strengths, we enjoy what we are doing, we do it better and we feel we are working toward our potential. Strengths psychologist, Alex Linley, defines a strength as "a pre-existing capacity for a particular way of behaving, thinking or feeling that is authentic and energizing to the user and enables optimal functioning, development and performance". In other words, identifying, activating and then using our strengths allows us to be our best selves. Research shows that when people use their strengths, they feel happier and more confident, are less stressed, more resilient and more engaged in their self-development. When combining our strengths with others and assisting them to use theirs, we build stronger and more co-operative relationships, enabling greater collaboration and teamwork.

CONNECT IT

Digital marketing and social media are essential elements in the modern business environment. Exponential technological growth in the last few years is marked and it impacts how businesses show up and keep on top of and in front of advancements and new platforms. Many senior leaders are not necessarily savvy in these areas. One CEO I worked with realized that his lack of skills in and understanding of the digital world was holding back the growth of his business and distracting him from focusing on what he was really good at. We did a scan of the leadership categories such as strategy, culture, innovation, operations, customer service, and finance and assessed where his strengths and interests were. He ended up realizing that by hiring a Chief Digital Officer for his senior team, the company would be better served. Not only was his energy freed up to focus on the big picture strategy for growth, but this leader also started expanding his skillset in the digital arena through the input from the new CDO. Creating a team around you with people who have complementary skills and expertise to augment the areas you aren't good at or perhaps that you don't even like shows leadership strength and will improve your impact. Awareness of the strengths you bring to the table is essential to effective leadership.

From a personal perspective, think about how you show up when you're visiting or having dinner with people you feel unconditionally accepted by, versus an obligatory event. In the first scenario, you are able to show up fully leading with your strengths and positivity, grounded in the shared values that shape this kind of trusted relationship. The dinner or the visit unfolds naturally. You feel vibrant, energized and at ease. Your best shines through and enhances everyone else's enjoyment of the experience. You don't even really have to think about it—your unique qualities and personality come to life naturally. In the latter scenario, think about how different the experience is. This could be a work obligation, a networking event or a function where you are seated with people you might not necessarily choose to spend the evening with. You might feel that the lack of alignment in ideas or approach creates misunderstanding, judgement or defensiveness. It is difficult to connect with your best in these situations or bring out the best in others. While clearly uncomfortable, these experiences also give us insight into our best by knowing the feeling of its opposite. Cultivating positive experiences, activating your strengths and being clear about the nature and context of these enable you to solidify and connect with what being at your best feels like and the positive impact it has on you, others and your environment.

APPLY IT

Best Self Exploration

This process is a key foundational piece and worth spending time on. There are four parts to be identified:

- your "best self story"
- your core values
- your key strengths
- your optimal energy points

Best Self Story

This exercise creates a way to better understand who you are at your best and what your best self feels like. You already have some information from the multiple perspectives feedback process in the previous chapter. The following adds additional insight.

Scan back and think about the movie of your life. Think about a time when everything was working—you were firing on all cylinders. Your strengths, skills, gifts and talents were all in play. You were excited to start the day—inspired to be your best and engaged in activities that supported that. It could be at any point in your life; high school, post secondary, early career or family life. What were the specifics of that story, that time in your life? Staying immersed in those memories take a moment to reflect on these questions:

- What was happening?
- What was going on around you?
- What were you doing?
- What strengths were you using?
- Who was in your life at the time?
- What kind of relationships were they?
- What was the quality and nature of your life at that time?
- How were you feeling?
- What values were present?

When you reflect on that time in your life, what resonates? What were the positive feelings you experienced? It is important to connect with not only the specifics of that peak time but also how you felt as a result of what you were living then. Also consider what values were present and what strengths were activated during this time in your life.

Core Values Identification

Being at your best is directly related to your values and their ability to flourish. Conversely, when your core values are being trampled or are not present, you are unable to show up at your best. Use your best self story to identify your top three to five values.

This core values inventory can be helpful to identify which values need to be present for you to be your best. Try not to overthink this—hone in on the ones that resonate most with you. There is no right or wrong in this exercise—only what fits for you.

Core Values Inventory

Abundance	Competition	Exhilaration	Inspiration	Personal Growth	Sensuality
Acceptance	Completion	Expansion	Integration	Persuasion	Serenity
Accomplishment	Conformity	Expert	Integrity	Planning	Service
Accuracy	Congruent	Faith	Intimacy	Playfulness	Sincerity
Achievement	Connection	Family	Intuition	Pleasure	Solitude
Action	Contemplation	Feeling	Invention	Power	Space
Adventure	Contentment	Flexibility	Judgment	Preparation	Spirit
Aesthetics	Contribution	Focus	Justice	Privacy	Spirituality
Alignment	Control	Forgiveness	Laughter	Process	Spontaneity
Altruism	Courage	Freedom	Leadership	Professionalism	Stimulation
Artistic	Creativity	Fun	Learning	Prosperity	Strength
Assistance	Dedication	Glamour	Love	Quest	Superiority
Attainment	Delight	Grace	Loyalty	Question	Synthesis
Augment	Dependable	Gratitude	Magic	Radiance	Tenderness
Authenticity	Devotion	Guidance	Magnificence	Realization	Thinking
Autonomy	Direct	Harmony	Mastery	Recognition	Thoughtfulness
Awareness	Discernment	Health	Movement	Refinement	Thrill
Awe	Discovery	Holistic	Mysticism	Reflection	Touch
Balance	Divinity	Honesty	Nature	Relationship	Transformation
Beauty	Drama	Honor	Nurture	Religious	Trust
Bliss	Dream	Hope	Openness	Resilience	Truth
Bravery	Educate	Humour	Orderliness	Responsibility	Understanding
Calm	Elegance	Image	Originality	Reverence	Uniqueness
Candor	Empowerment	Imagination	Partnership	Risk Taking	Unity
Choice	Encouragement	Improvement	Patience	Romance	Vision
Clarity	Energy	Independence	Peacefulness	Safety	Vitality
Comfort	Enjoyment	Influence	Perception	Satisfaction	Vulnerability
Commitment	Enlightenment	Information	Perfection	Security	Wealth
Community	Entertainment	Ingenuity	Performance	Self-Expression	Wholeness
Compassion	Excellence	Inquisitive	Perseverance	Sensation	Will

Strengths Identification

In addition to core values, you need to know your strengths and bring them to life to leverage them in your work and personal life. Think about the strengths that were activated in your "best self story". Use those as well as the following prompts to gain clarity and identify your top strengths. Think about:

Memories

- Going back as far as you can remember, what did you love doing? Do you still do it? Maybe even better than before? Do you still love it?

Activities

- What activities make you feel inspired and confident? At work? In your personal life? What comes naturally to you? What are you able to do well effortlessly?

Feeling States

- When do you feel at peace, excited, focused, most authentic?
- When do you feel jazzed? What are you doing, learning, experiencing?

Presence

- When are you really engaged in the moment—not worried about what just happened or what is next?

Think through and take note of what comes up for you when you think about those themes. Now complete the sentences below connecting with what you were engaged in and the associated feelings:

- When I was a kid, I loved to....
- When I feel jazzed...
- When I feel authentically me...
- When I feel calm and at ease...
- When I feel focused...
- When I feel inspired...
- When I sound passionate...
- When I am motivated...
- When I act effortlessly...

From thinking through the questions and completing the sentences, you can create a personal strengths inventory. Which top three to five strengths emerge? You can think about your strengths in general, as well as how they apply, or could apply, in the different areas of your life and work. What are your communication strengths, your strengths for providing direction or support for others? What are your strengths for decision making and judgment? What about your organizing, planning and problem-solving strengths?

Energy Points Exercise

In order to be at our best, we need to know and activate our strengths and positive emotions, as well as being grounded in our values. We also need to be energized and have an acute sense of where we get our energy, how we know when we are depleted and what we need to do to replenish our energy stores.

Jim Loehr and Tony Schwartz's work in their instructive book, *The Power of Full Engagement,* is impactful in understanding how to achieve our optimal frame of mind to be "fully engaged" in what we are being called to face. Their insights on the characteristics and importance of energy have impacted my coaching work for years and inspired me to create the five-point energy star model below.

The following exercise is a starting place to think about how the energy flow works and to help you identify how you get "filled" with respect to physical, emotional, intellectual, meaning and relational energy.

Use the five-point energy star as a way of thinking about your energy. What are the things that drive you in terms of each of the different energy points? What are the things that drain you? The energy flows in and out depending on not just what is happening but how it impacts you and how that makes you feel. Notice that there are also connections and relationships between the various energy points. If you are "full" in an energy point, what is the feeling state you achieve? You are in your optimal state when all points are at their max, feeding the centre core and metaphorically enabling the star to shine at its brightest.

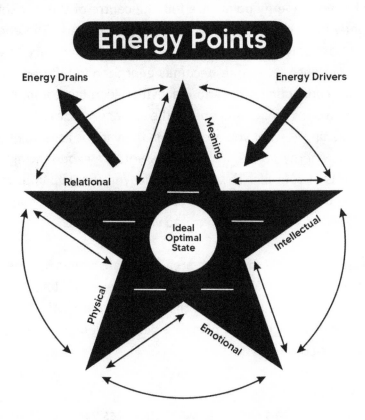

Our energy guides us, fuels us and is directly connected to the application of our strengths and the ability to live our values. If our values are able to flourish, our strengths are activated (and vice versa) and we are connected to the positive feeling states we strive to achieve. When we are fully energized, we are operating at our best.

Our energy points are connected to the physical, relational, emotional, intellectual and meaning components of our being. The star energy model offers a visual to show how our energy feeds our core and impacts our ability to show up fully inspired and present in our lives.

If all of your energy points are full, the centre of the star shines brightly and you are thriving in your life and work. The energy flows both ways which creates the up and down reality of your life experience. Everyone becomes energized in different ways, through connecting with various activities, learning, communities, roles or work. The life categories in the earlier exercise reveal "what is happening"—what you are doing in the various aspects of your life. The energy points are the "how you are experiencing" the elements of your life. This is about how you show up in terms of what you are engaged in—how energized or charged you are and how you actually feel in relation to your ideal state.

We also get depleted in each area at various points in time. We have to be acutely aware of the cues when we are getting depleted in any one of the points and then know what works for us in terms of re-energizing. To be at our best, all elements need to be functioning optimally:

- **Physical**
    - This relates to what energizes your body and also what needs to be present in your physical space for you to feel your best
- **Relational**
    - What needs to be happening in your relationships to feel full from an energy standpoint?

- **Emotional**
    - To feel emotionally at your best, what needs to be going on?
- **Intellectual**
    - To feel top of your game intellectually, what do you need to be engaged in?
- **Meaning (Spiritual or Purpose)**
    - For you to feel connected to your purpose, what has to be present? Note that I use the word "meaning" as sometimes people associate "spiritual" with religious. Use whatever word works for you in terms of connecting with your meaning energy.

In each of the five areas:

- What makes you feel optimal?
- What has to be present?
- What do you need to be doing?
- How do you know when you are being depleted in each area?
- What do you need to engage in to replenish? What works for you?
- Most importantly, what is the feeling state when your energy is optimal in each point? It isn't just a list of things to do and check off—it is actually articulating the feeling state to strive toward that enables you to be fully energized in each area.

Our overall energy also impacts how we show up in our lives from a reciprocal and "universe" standpoint. What we put out into the world from an energy standpoint is directly related to what we receive. Think about a person who always brings positive energy into a room, meeting or encounter. That positive energy is infectious. Alternatively, people who are depleted energetically pass on that sub-optimal vibe and can create a vicious cycle of negativity. What we exude, we attract.

Thinking through these exercises is not easy. I encourage you to stay with it, answer the questions and see what the components of your at your best profile are. It will serve you well!

Sometimes a life jolt can be all too consuming. Our best self can be covered up and inaccessible during challenging times. This is precisely the time to think through the exercises here and to intentionally access and get in touch with what "best" is for you.

COMMIT TO IT

CONNECT
WITH YOUR BEST

- What have you learned about who you are at your best?
- What are the feelings you experience when you are at your best?
- What is your "at your best" profile?
    - o Your top core values
    - o Your top strengths
    - o Your energy point components
- How can you cultivate and access your best more often?

Will you or won't you take action to connect with your best self?

CHAPTER 3

Befriend Imperfection

"There is a crack, a crack in everything.
That's how the light gets in."
Leonard Cohen

Once we intentionally enter into the research in our own life and connect with who we are at our best, we also have to embrace all of ourselves, which includes the imperfections. This needs to be done with honesty, vulnerability and without judgment. We need to be open to change where required, healing if necessary, and acceptance. Our cracks are part of who we are and when we have the courage to acknowledge them, we can get to know them and cultivate a healthy relationship with them.

Our imperfections and the elements of ourselves that seem to get in the way are just part of being human. There can be a tendency to be defensive, to ignore or to justify them. The people who achieve their best selves are those who have the courage to face the dark or shadow sides of themselves and use them as an impetus to become even better. Patterns are ingrained and defense mechanisms get in the way of forward movement. We can live in a stalled mode for a lifetime if we don't embrace the cracks. Choosing not to doesn't mean you can't lead a full life or be successful, but authentic happiness, peace, ease and reaching your full potential will typically remain out of reach.

People who don't fully grasp this concept remain stuck in their current level of development and are less likely to move toward becoming better.

This is about who we are when we are not at our best—the parts of ourselves that get triggered when we are threatened by circumstances, people or situations. These are the protective elements of who we are that can get activated when we experience a jolt. They can even create life jolts unknowingly. They can be our blind spots, or they can be the reactive parts of ourselves that emerge based on patterns, behaviours or thoughts. They most often don't serve us or the situation. They are the things that are triggered by our fear-based emotions. They are our ingrained, sometimes impulsive reactions that put us in "fight, flight or freeze" mode impacting body, mind and spirit. These are our insecurities, our behaviours, thinking and reactions when we are not at our best.

Tamara Levitt, Head of Mindfulness and Meditation Instructor at Calm, offers insight informed by a Japanese approach called *wabi sabi,* which is about not only embracing imperfections but also seeing the beauty in them. She describes the concept in terms of finding profound beauty in imperfection and celebrating things that are rough, authentic and modest. *Wabi sabi* offers a powerful lesson in acceptance. If we embrace our frustrations, self-judgement and flaws then step back to view the wider perspective of ourselves which also includes all our positive talents and qualities we then see the whole universe of who we are. Think about how we support our kids or our loved ones who come to us in a self-critical state of mind. We invite them to come to us whole with everything they consider imperfect, and we strive to show them the whole landscape we see—and we accept it all—attributes and weaknesses alike. The unique combination of all our traits, features and peculiarities make up who we are. This doesn't mean we don't strive to improve but it is about seeing and connecting to our uniqueness which supports our ability to own and offer "all of us" to the world in authentic and interesting ways.

We all develop defense mechanisms to protect ourselves from perceived criticism and hurt. Ego left unchecked can exacerbate our imperfections and stifle authentic self-confidence. We need our healthy ego to help balance us, ensure realistic self-perception and thus true self-confidence. However, we also need to be mindful of the fact that our ego can, at times, emerge dressed up as what we think is confidence but comes across to others as arrogance. We need the self-awareness to know when our ego is getting in our way.

While we need to be focused and connected to our strengths and who we are at our best, we also need to understand that as humans we are all perfectly imperfect. Gaining awareness of our cracks is an important part of the developmental journey. Through this awareness we can cultivate a relationship with our imperfections in order to empower ourselves and be in control of how we show up positively without being constrained by our weaknesses. Awareness is again a key theme that weaves its way through this work.

CONNECT IT

We have all experienced people and leaders who have blind spots when it comes to their imperfections. It may be someone you reported to or someone on your team. It could be someone who reports or reported to you. It's the example of the person who in spite of asking for feedback doesn't really listen. It's that person who hasn't really taken that honest look in the mirror and had the courage to see where their impact doesn't match their intention. They haven't been able to play out the movie in their mind in terms of what would happen if they actually took in the feedback and acted on it in service of greater impact or success. Instead, they get caught up in defending their position, wanting and needing to be right instead of effective. It is often unconscious. Not only can this cause stress for the leader, fuel divisiveness and block positive change and innovation, but it can also ultimately cost them their job or even their company.

In life outside work, our inability to own and understand our cracks can increase our stress levels. Think about planning a vacation. The planning stage can be a fun and meaningful experience, but oftentimes we can get in our own way, and turn the process into a stressful one. It could be that you get overwhelmed with too many ideas or that you want to please everybody. You could get tripped up by insecurity, perfectionism, control, ego or inflexibility. Think about how different it might be if you embraced and owned those tendencies and faced them differently. What if you accepted them, recognized that you can never please everybody—that there is no one perfect hotel, tour, restaurant or activity; that there are always more things to plan and do than there will be time for? What if you accepted that as a reality and viewed it as being OK? You don't need to be in control of all aspects of the trip. Not everyone is going to like all parts of what you planned and that's OK too. You can still plan anyway, without being overly wedded to your own ideas. While that trip may not be perfect as you intended, as no vacation ever is, it can still be a meaningful adventure and you can get on that plane with the perfectly imperfect plan, remain flexible, be present in each moment and enjoy it.

Inner Critic

We all have an inner critic that reminds us of our imperfections. It is the voice in our head that we have been hearing for much of our life. The voice that questions our decisions, tells us we are not enough, judges our actions and that wants us to believe we aren't good enough, worthy or that we cannot succeed and perhaps don't even deserve to. Everyone's inner critic is unique and specific. The inner critic lives and breathes by being right and pointing out flaws, but it only gains size and impact when we believe its message. By doing so, the inner critic becomes bigger and stronger.

- When does your inner critic show up?
- How big is your inner critic?
- What are the messages your inner critic tells you?
- When do you buy into those messages?

The goal is not to eliminate the inner critic completely, but to become aware of who your inner critic is. Your inner critic serves a function—to ensure you have thought things through, that you are challenging yourself, that you are living your values, that you are making best fit decisions and that you have the courage to step outside your comfort zone. The task here is to understand the dynamics of the power differential. Who is ultimately in control—you or your inner critic? If you can develop a relationship with your inner critic, you can shift the internal dialogue to become a two-way conversation instead of the inner critic simply dictating negative messages that you can become susceptible to believing.

APPLY IT

Personifying the Inner Critic

The best way to develop a relationship with your inner critic is to personify it. It is vital to get the voice out of your head and metaphorically "out there"—sitting across the table from you.

- Do you associate a gender with your inner critic?
- What is the tone of voice and pitch when your inner critic speaks to you?
- What physical form comes to mind when you think of your inner critic?
- What size is your inner critic?
- What colours come to mind when you think of your inner critic?
- What tangible symbols do you see when your inner critic emerges?
- What repetitive messages do you hear when your inner critic speaks to you? Make a list: you don't deserve that promotion, you aren't qualified, you aren't good enough, you will never achieve the goal, who are you to do this or that, you can't be a good parent, partner or boss... list specific examples.

- If you were to sketch a picture of your inner critic, what would it look like?
- When you look at your inner critic on the page in front of you what name comes to mind?

Once your inner critic is "out there", you can begin to develop and cultivate a new relationship. You can begin to speak back. What are your counter points to each of the critical messages you have become accustomed to hearing over the years? Connect with the tracks playing in your head that over time you have come to believe are the truth—become aware of them in a different way and practice interacting with them. What are the circumstances where your inner critic is loud and shakes your confidence? What do you want to say back? Experiment to see what is effective in quieting the inner critic's voice. Understand that the inner critic can only be strong, overwhelming and powerful if you allow it.

This exercise impacted me when I was doing my coach training program and has resonated with clients in a significant way over the years.

While the process I offer here, and in coaching my clients, is based on a future-forward perspective on growth and development, there is relevance in acknowledging where we have come from. This often involves revisiting and gaining perspective on the issues and experiences from your childhood that impacted the emergence and development of your inner critic. It is important to make the distinction between the coaching process and the therapeutic process. I am an advocate for both and often there is a place for both when someone is committed to personal growth and learning. If issues from the past, particularly themes from your childhood, keep tripping you up, that can be an indication that you would benefit from therapy as a supportive and helpful way to move forward.

It is important to acknowledge the younger self within each of us. Just as we want to develop a relationship with our inner critic, we also want to gain insight from reflecting on our younger self from our current adult perspective. We can't go back and change our experiences, but what we can do is choose what we learn from them and how we make decisions moving forward—because of or in spite of the experiences that shaped us. It is impactful to realize that our adult self can actually heal our younger self. It can be helpful to be curious about and interested in how our past has impacted us and how we can embrace the learnings from it. What are we holding onto? What do we need to forgive in ourselves and in others? What would our adult self like to share with our past self? How do we accept what was? We need to forgive ourselves and others to heal from our experiences. We also need to accept that we cannot compel others to take responsibility or even understand our version of the truth. Different people respond differently, even to the same context, especially children.

If we face the lingering wounds from the past and heal them, the scars that form are even stronger and more resilient than the original skin.

Younger Self Reflection

Think back to your first day at your first job. Recall the context, the environment, the people around you, the tasks on your to-do list as well as the range of feelings you experienced. Now imagine your current adult self approaching your younger self. The purpose of this internal conversation is to share the top strengths that you have identified in the wisdom gained through your life and work experiences. You share with your younger self the top three strengths that will provide confidence to show up fully on the job. Just as you are finishing sharing, your inner critic shows up uninvited. The inner critic is quick to downplay the three strengths and instead focuses on the one key thing that will continually trip up the younger self's ability to meet with success. Think about the roadblock or the key inhibitor your inner critic might bestow upon your younger self. Then, have your current wise adult self remind you of a fourth strength—the strength that rectifies the roadblock that the inner critic wants to consistently activate to get in the way of your success. What is the counterbalancing strength that you offer your younger self?

For example, when I work through this exercise I can identify my top strengths as effective communication, cultivating reciprocal relationships and the ability to achieve and help others achieve, inspired, successful results. My inner critic likes to remind me that, regardless of these drivers, my overthinking can get in my way every time. "Paralysis by over-analysis" is how I would describe it. Because this can be my tendency, I need to be aware of it. I also know that I have the ability to activate mindfulness to quiet my mind, ground myself and focus on what needs to be done and how I want to show up. Mindfulness is my fourth strength that I am constantly practicing and overlaying on the "spin" to avoid my key inhibitor, the complex thinking, from preventing me moving forward effectively. Learning to accept and work with my imperfection, while still a work in progress, serves me.

This exercise is a powerful way to identify the key message our inner critic presents. Once this is identified, the counterbalancing strength can be accessed and applied as needed. Experiment with this—be aware of this. Pay attention to how this recognition enables you to empower yourself and resist buying into the inner critic's version of you. Regardless of the key imperfection or weakness that trips you up, you do have the resources within you to challenge and work through them. Identifying and learning to activate this fourth strength intentionally is effective. Practice this.

Embrace the imperfections and shift the focus. You don't need to feel stressed and in the stranglehold of limitations from your past. You need to identify what depleted feels like so you can shift the experience of not being at your best.

Our minds have developed neural pathways in terms of response patterns. Think about how a gravel road over time develops tracks that cars gravitate to. The tracks, created by the reality of weather and wear, become the go-to path for vehicles travelling the road. It doesn't mean that new tracks can't be created. It does, however, mean that intention and different steering are required. We can change our patterns if we are aware of how we need to focus our energy to optimize the five-point star—so it is able to shine optimally. When we are triggered and depleted, we revert to patterns that we are used to even though they may not be ideal.

Owning all of you, which includes the vulnerability, the sadness, the pain, the grief and the imperfections is essential to move forward positively in life. Further, cultivating shifts in how you think, feel and act through intention and habits to create new pathways supports the creation of new directions that can better serve you.

You might be thinking, "I am who I am". I am successful and my patterns have got me to this place. You may be feeling resistance to acknowledging let alone embracing your flaws. This is a normal human response to protect yourself. However, there is wisdom in the adage, "what got you here won't get you there".

COMMIT TO IT

BEFRIEND IMPERFECTION

- What has your thinking surfaced about your imperfections and the nature of your inner critic?
- How can you empower yourself differently to overcome the internal messages that get in your way?
- What is the counterbalancing strength you can activate to move past the things that trip you up?

Will you or won't you take action to befriend and embrace your imperfections?

CHAPTER 4

Choose Your Mindset

*"Once your mindset changes, everything on the outside
will change along with it."*
Steve Maraboli

"Mind is a flexible mirror, adjust it, to see a better world."
Amit Ray

Once we have stepped into awareness, connected with who we
are at our best and embraced our imperfections in a way that
supports our development, we need to add the concept of mindset
to complete the foundation pieces for growth.

From a broad perspective, mindset is our predisposition to see
the world in a certain way, through a particular lens. The view is
always better from the high road!

How we view, think about and respond to life is determined by our
mindset and directly impacts our behaviours and actions. It isn't
so much what we see, but how we see it. This is always within our
control even if circumstances are not. We all have our patterns and

ingrained responses. Once we are aware of these, we can cultivate ways to shift them to increase our effectiveness and success.

"We cannot solve our problems with the same thinking we used when we created them."

Albert Einstein

If you don't understand the choices available to you in how you approach situations, you will be unable to create the best fit solution for what you currently face. You will remain stuck in terms of your ability to move to the next level, unable to successfully navigate the jolts and vulnerable to repeating past patterns that may not serve the situation.

Carol Dweck is well known for her description of two approaches to thinking—growth mindset and fixed mindset. A fixed mindset is when people believe their basic qualities, intelligence, talents and abilities are defined and unchangeable. People who have a growth mindset believe that potential, aptitude, and capacity can be developed over time through awareness, experience, mentorship and learning. Operating from a fixed mindset blocks successful navigation of life and leadership and creates reaction versus an intentional, planned response. Dweck's assertion is that talented people who find or create success have a growth mindset.

In a growth mindset, challenges are exciting rather than threatening and instead of feeling vulnerable or weak, those who possess a growth mindset are inspired about the opportunity to grow and stretch outside their comfort zone. The growth mindset focuses on the process, including the process that may have created a challenge or failure, and helps people to see things as learning opportunities and the chance to do better based on lessons learned.

Marilee Goldberg Adams talks about the inquiring or learner mindset versus the judger mindset. Her work on the power of asking questions is transformational. She invites people to identify how they are thinking about things on the mindset continuum and then to become aware of the kinds of questions they are asking. Here are some examples of questions based on the two mindset perspectives:

Judger Questions	**Learner Questions**
• What's wrong (about me, the other person, or the situation)?	• What's right (about me, the other person, or the situation)?
• Whose fault is it?	• What am I responsible for?
• How can I stay in control (or avoid going out of control)?	• What are my choices?
• How can I "look good"?	• What's useful about this? What can I learn?

It isn't about having one mindset or the other. We all encompass parts of each extreme and regardless of your inclination, neither is ultimately right or wrong. However, reflecting on your thinking style can support your growth, development and the achievement of successful outcomes. It is important not to judge yourself, even for the judging elements and instead shift to a curiosity frame of mind. When you find yourself judging either self, others or a situation, it is useful to flip to the learner questions and be curious about what else is possible in approaching the scenario.

The Link Between Mindset and Level of Development

When people see something, they attach meaning to it. Mindset is all about the way you see the world, what you notice and the meaning you ascribe to things. This occurs from your current developmental level. You show up in the world with the thoughts and actions you choose, and you relate to situations and to others based on the complex interplay of your mindset and your level of development.

The childhood development trajectory is well known and understood. Kids learn to walk, talk, think, reason, and reach developmental milestones within a particular time frame range. Typically, children move through these markers that are measured from birth to age 18 when, in the western world, we consider that they have moved through adolescence and attained adulthood. What is less well known is the fact that there is also an adult developmental pathway that is psychologically based. The difference is that not all adults progress through all aspects of this process. It isn't predetermined in the same way that childhood development is. This means elements of the adult maturation process may or may not be experienced by individual people. There are numerous phase and stage theories of psychological adult development that, while fascinating and well researched, are beyond the realm of this book. What is important here is that adults on the path of psychological development are continually evolving to different ways of seeing themselves, others, and the world. Think about watching in awe as babies become increasingly able to understand a wider world that is not just in relation to their specific, immediate needs. Similarly, the developmental path for adults leads to a broader perspective and deeper understanding of life's complexity and interrelationships.

A way to understand how we develop and increase our capacity for perspective-taking is shared by adaptive leadership expert, Ron Heifetz. He calls it "being on the dance floor versus being on the balcony". When you are at an earlier stage of development, you are "on the dance floor"—in the midst of the action, immersed in your own experience, dancing in the crowd and trying not to bump into other dancers. This is a subjective experience. If you move to the balcony and are looking down on the dance floor you are able to get a different perspective because of the view. Maybe you see that other dancers across from where you were dancing keep tripping over a crack or the area in which you were dancing was much more restrictive than a different part of the dance floor that was less crowded. This is a more objective experience of the same situation. As you grow and move through the stages of adult development, you can become increasingly objective and see more and more of the dance floor, by reaching higher "balconies" of observation and by developing the capability to move between different levels of balconies, even dipping back down to the dance floor when required. The beauty of accessing higher levels of development is that you get to bring all the previous levels with you and thus can hold a broad and deep perspective of yourself, others and the situation. It is about having a bird's-eye view of yourself and the world around you.

The vantage point visual below is an attempt to show how you see different things from the various viewpoints. Starting at level 1 when you are immersed "in" something and are "on the dance floor" you only see what is directly around you. As you approach level 2 you begin to see additional details. Moving to level 3 reveals more features and characteristics in terms of what is actually happening. Finally, as you attain level 4 you gain an even higher perspective and can see contextual details, such as the lines on the floor. At this point you are also able to move back and forth between the levels to uncover multiple perspectives and take in the complexities that were not apparent initially. Cultivating your ability to move from being "in" it to viewing a situation from multiple levels and perspectives expands your ability to see and understand the nuances, specifics, complexities and broader realities of a situation.

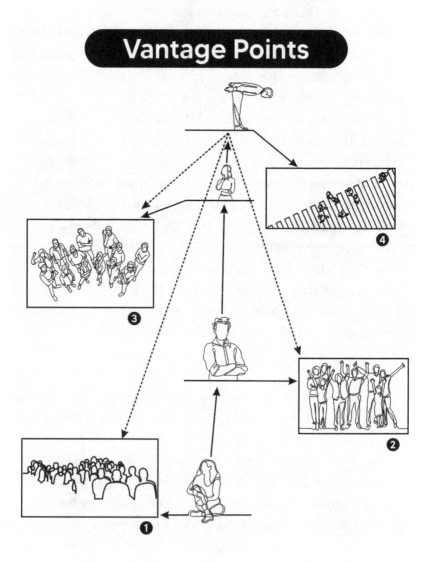

Developmental psychologist Robert Kegan's work is impactful in our quest to understand the way adults move toward increasingly higher order ways of making meaning as they mature psychologically. He coined the phrase "forms of mind" to describe the stages adults move through from a developmental standpoint. As you navigate your adult maturity, it's useful to understand what stage you are approaching your interactions from. Kegan describes how adults can move beyond being self-sovereign, a stage that makes sense of the world solely from the perspective of "self". This is when everything is seen from being "on the dance floor" metaphorically. When on the developmental journey you move through what he calls the socialized form of mind to self-authored and eventually self-transforming ways of seeing and being. You become increasingly objective and able to see and experience broader perspectives. You also become able to embrace complexity, paradox and become big enough to hold it all. Possibilities can be seen, curiosities explored, and new ways of showing up can be initiated. This development involves moving toward understanding things in relationship to others and being able to make choices based on those interrelationships. You become able to interact with and respond to the views others hold. Eventually, you can embrace and access increasing levels of impartialness that transforms how you make meaning because of the multiple perspectives and connections you now can consider. Holding polarities in the palm of one hand becomes possible.

Becoming aware and understanding where there is room to see what's possible and what mindset shifts could serve you is key to developmental growth. This will expand your capacity to think and respond to the world at a higher level from a psychological maturation perspective.

Think about looking something up on Google Maps. If you are zoomed right in on a location, you are able to see the detail and the specifics of the site. However, you can't plan the route to get there when you are zoomed in—you need to assess the situation and plot your path from a more distant view. By zooming out you are able to see the broader context, what is surrounding the location, how it fits with the wider landscape and how to chart your path. Then, the ability to zoom in and out creates an even fuller picture and understanding of the connections between the location and the overall environment.

David Petrie, in his journal article ,"The Mental Demands of Leadership Complex Adaptive Systems", uses a computer metaphor to describe the developing mindset inviting us to think about the leader's mindset as a personal operating system. In this scenario, next-generation apps and software that emerge require more complex structures to function than the current version of the POS system. Thus, the system itself needs upgrading for the new applications to work optimally. They can't just be downloaded and expected to run unless the operating system itself is enhanced. The same is true for a learner when faced with new information, concepts and ideas that can't necessarily be understood at the current level of development. Openness and cultivating new ways of thinking and being are required to develop expanded capacity.

Your mindset matters because it can either limit or liberate your potential. Your mindset and belief system affect everything in your life, from what you think and feel to what you do and how you react to the world around you. Succeeding is a state of mind—a journey not a destination. This knowledge and the subsequent undertaking to select the lenses that will support you in achieving your unique and specific life purpose is the key—and it is possible! To achieve success your mindset needs to match your aspirations, otherwise it will hold you back.

How are you thinking about your mindset now?
In what ways is it limiting you?
In what ways is it empowering you and enabling your growth?

How Can We Impact, Shift and Upgrade our Mindset for Increased Success and Well-Being?

It is one thing to understand the concept of changing and expanding one's mindset, but how do you actually do it? What is a more empowering mindset? How do you get there and not just think about it?

Because mindsets are deeply ingrained in our beliefs, we need to examine our belief systems and not be afraid to challenge them and explore other ways of thinking about things. We need to replace old patterns with new ones. Dweck talks about the brain as a muscle that grows stronger with use and that every time people stretch themselves to learn something the brain forms new connections and people can and do get "smarter" over time.

From a mindset perspective our view is not "how the thing is". It is, more accurately, "this is how I see the thing" and because "I see the thing in this way" it reinforces how I choose to act. If I try out—even as an experiment—to see the thing differently, what other possibilities will I see or experience? This is real learning in the broader sense.

When the pandemic first hit, I found myself seemingly clear that my facilitations could not effectively be offered virtually. I had developed and was facilitating a process for senior teams that was designed to be an in-person experience. My initial response to the sudden virtual world we were facing was that this program could not be effective if run via Zoom. That was my initial belief. Upon reflection I realized that this was only true because of how I was seeing it and that belief prevented me from moving forward with the contribution I was making to support organizational leadership. Once I became aware of this and intentionally opened up my thinking, I began to see different possibilities. I was then able to create online offerings that could effectively support leaders and organizations. I have also added creative ways participants can interact with the themes in a virtual format to inspire collaboration, learning and action.

Mindsets can change, but they tend to change slowly. So how do you upgrade your mindset for success? Again, the starting place for change is awareness, and understanding that your thinking can be adjusted.

There are three categories to consider in terms of shifting your mindset:

Actions—now that I see and understand my mindset vis-à-vis a particular situation, what do I want to do differently given the awareness I now have?

Experimentation—how can I experiment with different ways of thinking, acting and responding and be willing to let go of past patterns of behaviour?

Practice—what are the routines I can implement in my life and work to continually stretch and challenge my thinking and mindset to cultivate and re-enforce new, different and more effective results?

In thinking through the components relating to mindset and trying to understand the place you are coming from and where your want and need to go, consider the following:

- Awareness—make time to think because there is power in intention.
- Change your self-talk—focus on positivity and combating negative thoughts.
- Change your language—think in a "curiosity" or "question" mindset.
- Determine the mindset you need and act "as if" you had that mindset.
- Identify and address personal mental blocks.
- Learn and apply—read, be open, listen to podcasts and be curious about what else is possible.
- Get support, information and input from others.
- Surround yourself with people who share your desired mindset.
- Create new habits that support your mindset.
- Create compelling goals and re-visit them often.
- Focus on overall health—mind, body and spirit.
- Push yourself out of your comfort zone—resist being blocked by fear.
- Experiment with creativity—what other approaches can you explore? Engaging in visual or performing arts, whether as the artist or the spectator, is a powerful way to gain new perspectives that may expand your thinking and approach.
- Be courageous and inspired.
- Have confidence and believe in yourself and your ability to step into things differently.

This isn't just about intellectually understanding or learning things, but it is about evolving and integrating the learning, so we become different or better versions of ourselves because of applying what resonates. I invite you to infuse the development of different vantage points into your life in a way that works for you and impacts your decisions, actions, success and sense of well-being.

CONNECT IT

A great example of a leader with a fixed mindset is one who believes in traditional working hours and that being physically in the office is the only way to cultivate the highest productivity. While the pandemic has forced work from home, virtual interaction and flexible hours, many leaders still believe that the most effective structure is nine to five, Monday to Friday in the office as the "right" protocol and they can't wait to "get back to it". Leaders who operate from a growth mindset are in a continual state of assessing what works in terms of our current reality. This open-minded perspective creates the kind of thinking likely to culminate in a hybrid work model. Such a win-win is better aligned with creative solutions and rules of engagement resulting in even greater employee commitment and productivity. Further, a leader with an open mindset is better able to pivot products and services to meet the demands of the complex market conditions in our ever-changing globalized world. The examples are numerous over the past year: the organization that has gone straight to the consumer to circumvent the supply chain challenges, the product that has been repurposed to meet current needs or the delivery model that has shifted to online due to bricks and mortar closures or any other number of potential innovations we are experiencing during and because of the pandemic.

When faced with any number of personal situations, whether positive or negative, including things related to marriage, engagement, a new home, pregnancy, a new role, graduation planning, a health diagnosis, relationship crisis, death, miscarriage, job loss, financial difficulty, who do you choose as your go-to people? They are typically the ones who you know are open, curious and will see and hear you. They are the people who will brainstorm possibilities and embrace thinking creatively about all the options. They will encourage you to seek out and achieve your potential, forging the best possible path forward. They will support and push you outside your comfort zone, believing in your ability. You go to them because you know that they won't judge you or impose rules or "shoulds" that may not be right for you. That open, curious mindset enables you to view the situation in a way that serves you. It is powerful and empowering and the proof lies in the fact that you seek out this perspective.

APPLY IT

Try this Mindset Self-Assessment. Take a few minutes and think about where you tend to dwell, where your go-to place is on this continuum. Make note on the line for each polarity. Think about which mindset qualities best describe your tendencies, patterns and the way you view things. Think about the fixed and growth mindsets as the big picture lens. The other descriptors are ways to break the concept of mindset into more specific approaches so you can be more detailed in your understanding of how you view things.

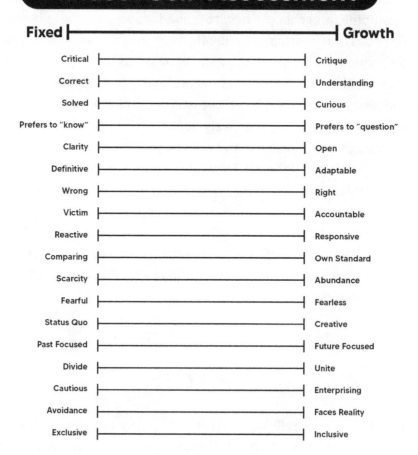

Mindset Self-Assessment

Fixed ⊢————————————————————⊣ Growth

Fixed		Growth
Critical		Critique
Correct		Understanding
Solved		Curious
Prefers to "know"		Prefers to "question"
Clarity		Open
Definitive		Adaptable
Wrong		Right
Victim		Accountable
Reactive		Responsive
Comparing		Own Standard
Scarcity		Abundance
Fearful		Fearless
Status Quo		Creative
Past Focused		Future Focused
Divide		Unite
Cautious		Enterprising
Avoidance		Faces Reality
Exclusive		Inclusive

Once you have considered where your preferences and tendencies land on each line, take a minute to notice the patterns. What do you see? What can you learn about your mindset? Which ones relate to what you are currently facing? Where would it serve you to focus? What would ideal be? Which ones work well for you? Which ones get in your way? What could be possible for you?

One of the CEOs I worked with realized after doing this exercise that she tended to lean toward clarity and "solving things" in spite of the fact she saw herself as very open-minded. As a result of this awareness, she decided to add a "self check in" when making decisions to ensure she resisted the temptation to act too quickly to get things done without specifically reaching out and considering a variety of alternatives. While a relatively small change in her planning process, it made a difference in her ability to reach better and more creative outcomes.

You might be thinking that not everyone has a choice and that can be true for many elements of a jolt. You might be thinking personalities are fixed, that the way you think about things has worked so far, or that the stage in life you are at means that things are set in stone. You might also be thinking that this is just too much work so you should instead just focus on the immediate things. You have no time to think about things this deeply let alone act on them. You may be committed to your past patterns that have enabled you to be successful. So why wouldn't you just repeat the cycle? The ideas offered here in terms of mindset and your level of development have hopefully inspired you to think further about these concepts and be curious about embracing them and trying to weave them into your thinking, feelings and actions—even as a pilot project to see what else may be possible for you.

COMMIT TO IT

CHOOSE
YOUR MINDSET

- What mindsets do you tend to gravitate to?
- What developmental level are you operating at?
- How can you tap into other ways of thinking about things that will help you move forward and question the patterns that hold you back?
- How can you approach your situation from different vantage points and with a curiosity mindset?

Will you or won't you take action to choose your mindset?

SECTION B

And Just Like That

"Life is either a daring adventure or nothing. To keep our faces toward change and behave like free spirits in the presence of fate is strength undefeatable."
Helen Keller

We have explored the foundations for growth which include:

- Paying attention intentionally to raise awareness
- Connecting better with who you are when you are at your best
- Understanding, accepting and befriending your imperfections and
- Choosing your approach and mindset

Now we can move to the next stage to explore how we can meet the jolts and prepare ourselves for navigating the transition.

Because we are always metaphorically living in our own equation, we know what it feels like when a variable changes. And Just Like That, the solved equation we were enjoying is no longer our reality. When this happens, it is time to circle back around to examine not only what the new variables are but also what the implications are and what new question or questions we need to ask ourselves.

These are the moments when everything shifts. It can be a long time coming, it can be something you hoped for and planned... or it can hit you out of the blue. Whatever the particular context and circumstance, it requires you to shift your thinking, your actions, your life... Just Like That.

I have mentioned it before, but I want to emphasize that these shifts, these changes in our variables, can be positive or negative, internally generated or externally imposed, large or small and also can be the beginning of an ongoing reality. Regardless of the quality, size or nature these circumstances call us to respond.

The And Just Like That moment actually happens at two points in time. It happens when the jolt hits—or when we realize that something has changed or has to change. It also happens at the other end, when a solution, positive outcome or direction arrives. And Just Like That emerges from the work–the thinking, the searching, the experimenting. You can't plan exactly for the Aha moment, but you will know it when it arrives. It is when you become clear about what you need to do, where you need to go, and who you need to become.

The next two chapters explore the impact and implications of the jolt and then Section C addresses the process that cultivates the conditions for the moment of clarity to emerge at the other end—Just Like That.

CHAPTER 5

Embrace the Jolts

"Things falling apart is a kind of testing and also a kind of healing. We think the point is to pass the test or to overcome the problem, but the truth is that things don't really get solved. They come together and they fall apart. Then they come together again and fall apart again. It's just like that. The healing comes from letting there be room for all of this to happen: room for grief, for relief, for misery, for joy."
Pema Chodron

"It's not the load that breaks you down,
it's the way you carry it."
Lena Horne

Life challenges are inevitable—they are part of the journey. Recognizing when we are at a turning point is vital. We have to know when a variable in our life has changed, which at times is easy and at other times is more subtle or even emerges without us being aware. Acknowledging and understanding that we need to pivot in some way enables us to begin to plan, strategize and move toward the next step. We want to embrace the jolt in the belief that it can serve our ultimate goal of increased happiness, ease and success in our life and work. Even in cases where it is extremely painful, sad and challenging, we need to remain hopeful and believe in the process.

We can also be challenged by positive jolts. Think about getting the promotion you always wanted, getting married or moving in with your partner, buying a new house, having a baby, becoming a grandparent, hearing a positive health diagnosis, moving to the city you always wanted to live in, or buying the business that has long been your dream. These things require us to plan our lives and approach differently even if they bring energy and excitement. The process of awareness, reflection and who we want to be is the same as it is for the difficult jolts. If we want to ensure that how we show up and how things evolve are in alignment with what our ultimate goal is and with how we want to be and feel in the new life equation, it is essential to step into the process with as much intention as ever. This will increase our chance of things working out the way we want in terms of achieving satisfaction, success and happiness.

Life is complex and unfortunately we can't organize our lives in a way to avoid the jolts. What we can do, however, is learn how to view and meet them differently, by seeing jolts as a catalyst for growth and using them in service of what we want. If we embrace, choose to respond and invite them onto our path in a different way, we increase our chance of successful navigation.

The bottom line is that if you don't get this, you can't meet the jolts in a way that serves you, whether they are positive or negative. You will be moving against the flow of your life, with all the effort and strain that requires, instead of going with it. Being in resistance mode increases stress, anxiety and blocks your ability to access the qualities, skills, gifts and strengths in ways that support successful navigation and resolution. Left unattended or unchecked, the stress response (fight, flight, freeze) not only negatively impacts the situation you are facing, but also your physical and mental health. It can also leave you vulnerable to being a victim of circumstances instead of an empowered driver of solutions.

And Just Like That, something changes in your life. That jolt, challenge or issue, regardless of its source or size, is before you, requiring attention. In addition to jolts that eventually are resolved there are also things that represent ongoing jolts. These are the chronic sorrows. These are the ones you can learn to manage in the best way possible, but that you carry with you in some way throughout your lifetime. Any jolt changes the variables in your life components and impacts your current life equation. They need to be addressed. They challenge you and force you into a transition of some kind. Jolts represent a reordering of what you have come to know as the status quo in your leadership and life.

Despite what people share or how they present themselves I can tell you that after having the privilege of almost 20 years of coaching leaders, which has fostered many very close and unique relationships, people experience an incredible range of "stuff"— from extreme highs to extreme lows. "Stuff" happens in every category of life and often the specifics and complexities straddle more than one category.

The jolts can occur in any of the life categories, including among other things the following:

Livelihood or Career
- Sudden job loss
- Intentional job change
- Retirement
- Achieving a promotion or a new role
- Losing a key team member
- Changes in your industry

Personal Development
- Getting or not getting into a program or credentialing process
- Starting, succeeding at, or being prevented from a continuing education process, a new habit, routine or practice
- Being impacted by what you are reading, learning, watching, listening to

Finances
- Financial success and the decisions involved with safeguarding that
- Estate planning, retirement goals and decisions or issues that impact your budget
- Stock market shifts
- Financial hardship or bankruptcy
- Financial implications from divorce
- Financial responsibility to others (kids, parents, loved ones in need)
- Changes impacting your organization's finances or targets

Health and Wellness
- Health scare or diagnosis (self or others)
- A healing experience or catalyst event that spurs a wellness initiative or lifestyle change

- Injury
- An emotional jolt that impacts your mental health or someone you care about
- Addiction
- Sleep challenges
- Accident (self or others)

Fun

- Loss of access to these activities (pandemic)
- No time to devote to "fun"
- Engaging in a new activity
- Loss of the ability for any number of reasons to engage in these activities
- Implications of committing to new activities or re-connecting to activities you have previously enjoyed

Social Life

- Activities, events, get-togethers, destinations, venues, clubs
- Loss of access to social and leisure activities (pandemic)
- Implications of intentionally establishing new elements in this category

Family

- Relationship jolts and shifts
- Kids leaving home
- Challenges with spouse
- Marriage or divorce
- Someone in your family circle experiencing a jolt or challenge
- Birth
- Death

Home
- Moving
- Renovating
- Being evicted or losing your home
- Ability to access travel (or not)
- Connecting to natural environments (or not)

Creativity—Committing to pursuits in creative endeavours (which can impact other areas of life) or being prevented from being able to continue these due to illness, injury or changes in circumstances
- Music
- Art
- Painting
- Poetry
- Dance
- Writing
- Other creative expressions

Relationships—work, social, peripheral
- Cultivating new ones
- Circumstances that shift relationships with friends, colleagues, mentors, peers, acquaintances
- Boundaries around current ones
- Enhancing relationships
- Letting go of ones that don't serve you

The jolts can require situational fixes, significant life structure change or they can mean fundamental ongoing shifts in how you navigate and experience your life. They range in size and impact depending on your particular situation.

As mentioned, there is also a category of challenge that can be ongoing and pervasive. These are the jolts that we need to learn to carry with us gracefully—the chronic sorrows, grief due to loss of a child or a loved one, the ongoing responsibility of leading an organization, navigating the world and family life with a child with special needs or learning differences, supporting loved ones who struggle with addiction, mental health issues or are living with a chronic health condition. Living with and navigating these kinds of challenges with grace, love and radical acceptance weave through the fabric of our lives and define who we are and who we can become as a result of embracing our reality.

Pervasive challenges can strengthen how we bring our best self forward and can add depth and richness to the quality of our character. They can positively impact the way we walk on this planet if we choose to approach them from a place of true acceptance. I am not suggesting that these challenges are easy—rather, they can be excruciating and filled with greater ups and downs than other jolts or other people's circumstances. However, I do believe that the principles we are talking about, if applied, can be supportive. When we intentionally craft our life to capitalize on what is possible in our particular circumstance, we can become the victor instead of the victim.

The reality is, when we are faced with jolts, by definition they switch up the rhythm of our life. They knock us off balance and force us out of our regular routines. We are forced to re-examine our beliefs about success and failure. The life equation we are living is no longer relevant or our reality. We are required to understand the new and emerging landscape, identify the implications and the new variables to create the new question we are being called to step into, work through and solve—for now.

It is important to cultivate your own luck and make your own opportunities. There is a book called *Good Luck* written by Alex Rovira and Fernando Trias de Bes. It is a parable that highlights how "good" luck (as opposed to simply luck) is really when preparedness meets opportunity. Relating this to the context we are working through, you can do things intentionally to position yourself to respond to jolts in a positive and productive way. In essence, creating your own good luck.

An example is someone facing the rejection of getting into a desired program. They can view this as defeat or they can make a plan to get what they want in another way or create a Plan B as an even better solution than what they had initially wanted. The point is, there is always another way. We can lament that what we wanted didn't turn out the way we imagined, or we can have the courage to be curious about the meaning we can make from it, focus on what we can cultivate, and thus what emerges can fit with our skills, gifts and experiences in a more impactful way.

CONNECT IT

It's important to think about and apply examples that are both positive and negative, particularly from a business perspective. I've often been engaged by clients who are actively seeking a positive career change or promotion. I'm reminded of a client who wanted to be coached to capitalize on her leadership skills and take her career to the next level. The goal was to become a CEO. Once she achieved the role, her focus quickly turned to embracing and becoming all that she envisioned an effective CEO to be. It was a positive change, but it required grounding, intention and continual checking in with how her intentions and goals actually came to life when applied to the new organization she was leading. It also required a reorganization of her personal life, especially in the initial months.

I was in awe of her ability to be patient with herself and the existing senior executive team she inherited. Her commitment to following through on her first 90-day plan, her ability to be honest and cultivate a realistic assessment of what was working and what would be better was impressive. This ultimately led to a successful transition and culminated in her becoming an impactful CEO who, within her first year, increased employee engagement markedly, effectively restructured the Senior Leadership Team, and increased market share significantly. While it appeared seamless, it took tenacity, reflection, and focus to turn the organization around in the span of only a year! Her success came from having a clear vision of what kind of firm but fair leader she wanted to be and then set up the structures and support to get there. This included establishing consistent feedback loops with her team, regular accountability check-ins within the 1-1 Executive Coaching structure, joining a CEO peer learning group, and establishing a daily early morning planning and review time to stay on top of what was actually happening progress-wise. She had the courage to do the work to make it happen.

Effective leadership is not only measured by the successes of a leader, but also by how they navigate challenges. These can include how leaders respond when one of their top executives resigns, or how leaders in the industries most hit by the pandemic have owned and embraced what they have been forced to deal with. Or what about the leader whose business is significantly impacted by increased competition, or the company whose bottom line is impacted by the online presence of a start-up or by the superior technology of those operating in their space? Taking radical responsibility for these, or the multitude of other challenges leaders face regularly is vital. Leaders who are responsive, open minded and resourceful in their approach to challenges set themselves up to achieve optimal outcomes despite being tested by the jolts.

Personally, we can all relate to various jolts both negative and positive in our lives and think about how effectively we navigated and embraced them. The sorrow of death is part of life's reality and of course the ultimate excruciating jolt. When faced with the death of a loved one in order to eventually manage, carry and live with our grief we need to feel all the feelings and then gradually move forward one tiny step at a time. The pain is deep, real and can be enduring with no predetermined timeline, yet unending suffering does not have to be the lasting destiny.

At the other end of the life cycle, new babies entering the world rises to the top in terms of positive impact—whether that makes you a parent, an aunt, an uncle, a grandparent or any other special connection to the promise of new life. While this is the ultimate positive jolt or life change, if we don't embrace it in all of its complexity and all of the polarities surrounding it, we aren't setting ourselves up for success. This incredible arrival invites us to think about our role, our relationships and how we want to show up in terms of our particular connection, especially as a parent with all the hope and excitement as well as the responsibility.

When we are jolted open it changes us and potentially reveals who we really are.

The point is to use the jolt as a springboard to the next level of growth. It is necessary to see jolts as a new chapter in your life narrative, whether they immerse you in joy or sorrow or a mix of both. It is important to think about what happiness and joy even mean to you. We all have different things that resonate in terms of what ideal looks and feels like. I particularly appreciate the poet Ross Gay's thoughts. He talks about how people describe joy and how it connects to happiness. His interpretation of joy is that it is informed by the profound sorrow that we're always in the midst of. The joy he is interested in he calls "adult joy", and it is more than just happy. This suggests that the joy and happiness we strive for is actually mixed with a range of emotions and the goal is to hold it all simultaneously and be at peace.

APPLY IT

Review Your Jolts Exercise

Scan the movie of your life and think about the main jolts—positive and negative. Think about each experience and then ask yourself the following four questions for each one:

- What happened?
- What did you do?
- What emerged?
- Who did you become as a result?

As you look at what you recalled for each instance when answering these questions, what themes and patterns do you notice? How can the process you used in the past be overlayed on the present?

Where were your strengths applied successfully and how can they be activated now? Based on your reflection what do you want to avoid? How do the ways you responded in the past inform how you might think about what you now face? What worked? What template could you create for yourself to effectively deal with your current situation?

Things happen in life and sometimes it is easy to slip into the belief that you have no control over it anyway, so why not just keep your head down and keep going. Compartmentalizing, avoiding, or ignoring are also easy states to fall into. There can be the overwhelming feeling that so much energy is required just to get through the day to day that there isn't any energy left, or that there is just too much on your plate overall, never mind your never ending daily to do list. You might think it is best to just power through. Even when the jolts are positive these tendencies emerge, you get caught up in the inertia and don't pause, step back and really think about how this particular shift will best be embraced and integrated into your life. However, it is worth taking the time to do the work. It will enable you to use the jolts in service of yourself and your life.

COMMIT TO IT

EMBRACE THE JOLTS

- What is the current shock, jolt, change, surprise, shift or challenge and what elements of your life is it impacting?
- How does it relate to your thoughts, feelings and behaviours?
- When you review how you have successfully navigated jolts in the past what patterns do you see?
- How can you use what has worked in the past to inform how you can proceed in this situation?
- How can you shift your thinking to see this as an opportunity to become even better?

Will you or won't you take action to meet and embrace your current life jolts?

CHAPTER 6

Take on the Transition

"Change is situational. Transition, on the other hand, is psychological...We resist transition not because we can't accept the change, but because we can't accept letting go of that piece of ourselves that we have to give up when and because the situation has changed."
William Bridges

Understanding the transition process and what is going on beneath the change that any challenge requires is vital. I want to make a distinction between change and transition. I am not talking about a model of change per se, which involves setting a goal or clarifying a vision, identifying steps and implementing a plan in order to reach the goal. While this is part of it, transition is about what is occurring underneath the surface—the process that is happening whether or not we are aware of it. Learning about the transition process and the specific ways we need to think about whatever change we are facing can guide the next right action in support of successful implementations and goal achievement. We can become better equipped to navigate through the issue to solve the equation. Knowledge is power, thus, if we understand the underlying realities and corollary considerations, we are more empowered to meet the challenge, change or opportunity. It isn't just the impact of the jolt, but also all the elements of our work and life that may be affected. I want to provide you with a template, an approach and a way of thinking about transitions so you are better able to plan and execute your own successful transition.

If you don't step into the transition process with intention, situations can happen to you instead of being able to manage them. You will also be vulnerable to getting stuck and unable to let go of what was—even if it is something that you wanted to change. Even if you can create the vision of what you want next, you will have difficulty getting there if you don't understand the components of the transition process, thus inciting further complexity on top of the jolt.

Jolts force change and initiate a transition process whether you like it or not. They change one or more variables in your life equation. Again, you need awareness, and you need to pay attention to what is really going on. Not what you wish for, hope for or had planned for. Radical acceptance is required. By this I mean not just intellectually knowing or understanding that something is happening but truly embracing "what is" regardless of whether or not it is wanted or ideal. This enables an unfolding instead of engaging in a fight against what needs to be faced. Then you need to step into the process of what's next, what you want, what you can create and what is possible given the reality.

When life hits you with a jolt, or you initiate one, change is required. The evolving transition accompanies the change. There is a shift in what you have come to know as your truth, so now what? How do you respond to these instead of letting them control you?

William Bridges' work is foundational to our understanding of these concepts from a personal and organizational perspective. His work underpins much of the coaching work I have done over the years, and I recommend any of his books for anyone interested in a deeper look.

A helpful way to view the relationship between change and transition is to think about moving. When you decide to move, you enter into a change process. You think about where you want to live, the city, the neighbourhood, the community. You decide what kind and size of home you want—whether it is a house, condo or apartment. Then you set out to explore the various options until you key in on the ideal choice for this particular time in your life. Let's look at a situation where you are successful in getting the home you want, then you move in. The change has happened, but that is not the end—it is really just the beginning of the transition process. Does the new home live up to your expectations? What are the surprises? What is the impact of the new commute to work? Or are you working from home and how does the new space lend itself to this reality? What is the fit with the neighbours? The community? What are the things you hadn't thought through—the need to find a new doctor or dentist? What are the new routines required for shopping—where are the grocery stores or the drug store? How does the new reality impact the logistics of your life? You may find yourself grieving the loss of old neighbours while at the same time feeling excited about meeting new people. Your kids may have intense feelings about changing schools or your partner may be having second thoughts. Any combination of things can be occurring simultaneously. It is complex. These things can all work smoothly or they can include challenges or shifts you hadn't thought through. This is the transition part of change.

The process of transition is occurring whether or not you are aware of it. It is the psychological process that occurs beneath the specific change.

We tend to think that when one thing ends another begins. The reality is that there is a whole phase in between the two. This is the "in-between", the chaotic time of "I don't know". It takes courage to really be in, navigate and stay in this phase for as long as it takes for the new beginning to emerge.

I created the following model to help people understand the psychological process and components of transition and thus to increase their chance of successful navigation.

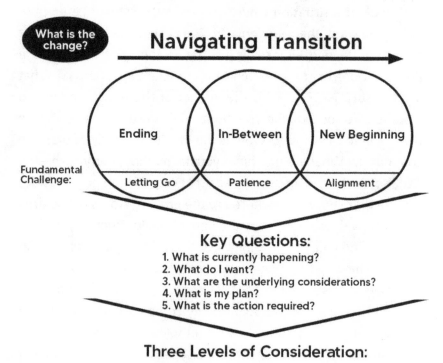

Key Questions:
1. What is currently happening?
2. What do I want?
3. What are the underlying considerations?
4. What is my plan?
5. What is the action required?

Three Levels of Consideration:
1. Self
2. Others/Team
3. Bigger Context/Organization

As highlighted in the above model, there are three phases of transition. Each phase has a corresponding fundamental challenge that needs to be considered and addressed for successful navigation. They are highlighted as follows:

Phase	Challenge
• The Ending	• Letting Go
• The In-Between	• Patience
• The New Beginning	• Alignment

With respect to endings things can end abruptly or the ending process may have been coming for quite some time. As parents, we know that our kids leaving home is coming and we prepare for it for years. We may have wanted our company restructured to make it more effective or the team may have wanted a new leader. We may have been wanting to leave our job for a while, and perhaps have even been planning our exit or we may have been actively looking for a buyer for our company. Perhaps the ending comes out of the blue and we are asked to leave our role. Whether the ending is something we want or not—it always requires new ways of thinking and being. Life as we know it will end and there is loss involved—even if "what was" wasn't working for us, or even if we have been actively working towards the ending in anticipation of the new beginning. The fundamental challenge of the ending, whatever it may be, is letting go.

Letting go is about grieving what was, being aware of what we are leaving behind and embracing all the emotions and realities that are connected to that. Grief is like a boulder. Initially it is overwhelming, so large that it blocks every movement, thought and action. Over time we gradually chip away at it—thoughtfully, patiently—until eventually it becomes small enough that we can pick it up, put it in our pocket and carry it with us.

The pandemic is a clear example of an abrupt ending on a global level—a shared experience of a collective ending and collective grief. Everything we knew about best practices in leadership, our industries, how we balanced work and family life changed almost overnight. Even our kids attending school came to an end. The entire structure of our work and personal lives was and still is impacted.

Once something ends, you enter into the "in-between", the "don't know"—don't know where I am going, don't know how I will get through this, don't know if it is the right thing, don't know why this is happening, don't know if the timing is right, don't know if this is really what I want, don't know how it will work out. This is a confusing and scary time. We are being called to respond, to shift our thinking, to plan differently, yet there are so many uncertainties. Even if we are clear about where we want to go and what we want the new beginning to look like, there is a chasm between here and there. We are anxious to land the new job, start the next opportunity, triumph over the health challenge, move to the next city or home, complete the accreditation, go on the next travel adventure or be in the new relationship. This period is best navigated if we know, understand and embrace it, if we truly enter it with a mindset of curiosity and possibility. We are supposed to feel uncertain at this stage and we need to be patient with ourselves, others and the process.

Patience is the fundamental challenge at the in-between phase of the transition process. This stage causes acute discomfort, particularly for bright, successful people who have achieved a lot in their lives and careers. You want answers—you want to implement and move forward confidently. This makes sense yet you have to resist the temptation to move too quickly. If you miss something, the implementation has a lower chance of being impactful. You can't rush yourself or those around you through this phase. It can be an up and down process—but knowing that ensures preparedness. Everyone involved needs to stay in and tolerate the uncertainty in order to move through it. And, unfortunately, the only way through is through!

The goal is to navigate the in-between and move toward the new beginning with intention and clarity. The start of something new doesn't ensure that everyone involved, even including yourself, is there yet. The fundamental challenge of the new beginning is alignment. Does what you are stepping into align with what works currently? You may have strategized and planned but once you begin is it what you imagined or hoped for? Is it what you really want? Does it achieve what you set out to create or step into? What needs to be adjusted so the new beginning actually works and is the ideal?

Another characteristic of the transition process is that it is not linear. You can dip in and out of the stages, moving back and forward on your journey at various points in time depending on how you are responding and how you are experiencing your reality at a particular point in the process. You may change your mind about pursuing the new job, convincing yourself that the current one is fine. You may try again to stay in the relationship that isn't working because the fear of being alone is too overwhelming. You may revert to old patterns in work and life because they are comfortable, and the uncertainty of the change is daunting. You may also fast forward to new beginnings prematurely and realize that the decision wasn't the right one. Impatience can get in the way of successful new beginnings. All of this is normal and is part of the complex process of transition.

In addition to the fundamental challenges at each phase—letting go, patience and alignment—each has three levels of consideration.

Self—how are you personally interacting with the change or transition? How are you thinking about it? What are you choosing? How are you navigating it? What is in your control and what is not?

Others—how are you leading and supporting the others involved (team, family)? What are the conversations you are having? How do you need to shift the way you message things? What do you need to focus on depending on who you are communicating with? What are the processes you are implementing? Where are others connected to the change at in the transition process?

Bigger context—what is the connection and what are the implications to the organization? The community? The world? What is the narrative? What are the rules of engagement? How are you communicating the reality? How are you receiving feedback from the broader context to apply to the transition?

The pandemic is a relevant example here. We have our individual responses to it and then we have the responses of our teams at work and families at home, as well as our interpretations of what is happening on a global level. We are collectively grieving and experiencing change and transition. We are actively engaged in the chaos of the unknown. We are not at the new beginning yet and in fact we can't even imagine what it looks like even though we are trying to envision it and plan for it. We are experiencing the inevitable ups and downs, all in the somewhat dark and chaotic in-between place trying to figure it out. We are being called to stay balanced, focused and optimistic in the midst of unprecedented uncertainty. Not an easy task, but one made easier if we normalize the experience from a human and psychological perspective.

So, as you move through the transition, this one or any transition you may be facing in your work or your life, you need to ask five fundamental questions at each stage and with respect to each level of consideration (self, others, the bigger context):

1—What is currently happening?
- Not what you wish were happening, not what was supposed to have happened, not what you deserve, but what is actually happening?
- What are the components of the current situation?
- Questions for each phase:
  - Ending—what is ending? What do you need to let go of? What has been let go for you?
  - In-between—what have you lost? What are the uncertainties, the chaos, the fears? What are you excited about?
  - New beginning—is it what you want? Is it what you hoped for? Imagined?

2—What do I want?
- Ending—whether an ending you initiated or not, how do you want to show up? What do you want and need to let go of?
- In-between—what do you want during this phase? How will you be patient with yourself? What are the habits and practices that you will engage in to be able to adequately process what you are going through? How do you stay balanced when things are uncertain? How will you evaluate and process what you are learning and

experiencing? What do you want or need to do or try to get through this stage?

- New beginning—how do you envision the "movie in your mind" of what you want? The next best role, the best fit company, the new relationship or the next iteration of the current one, the best fit home, city or country. What is the goal not just in terms of what you want but also in terms of who you want to be and how you want to feel?

3—What are the underlying considerations?

- The thoughts, feelings, emotions and other elements occurring beneath the surface at each stage.
- How do you want to show up?
  - Ending—how are you feeling about what is ending?
  - In-between—what is in your control? What is not? How is it impacting your energy points?
  - New beginning—does this align with what you wanted? Does this feel ideal? Any what ifs?

4—What is my plan?

- Given what you want, how will you map it out?
  - Ending—what is your plan for closure? How will you communicate to stakeholders?
  - In-between—what structures can you put in place to stay in it or to move through it? How will you create and communicate structure for others involved?
  - New beginning—what is the plan for navigating and creating the new beginning and how you will get there?

5—What is the action required?

- Ask yourself what thinking, learning, conversations and actions you actually need to do at each stage: ending, in-between, new beginning?

These questions need to be asked often and at different stages. The process is in motion and the questions help determine where you are and what needs attention in order to reach an aligned new beginning.

CONNECT IT

An example of the importance of understanding the phases of this process comes from my work with a telecommunications company several years ago. The senior leader I was working with had a great vision for staying ahead of the changes in the industry and set out to rebrand his part of the business. His enthusiasm was inspiring, and he created a whole new brand strategy that involved updating many elements of the business including the logo, territories and the way the sales reps worked together and were compensated. He was excited about the well-researched and thought-out strategy that he believed addressed many of the things that hadn't been working for the team and the larger parent organization. He enlisted my coaching support to help him figure out why the changes weren't being embraced by his people. As we explored what was actually happening it became apparent that while he unveiled changes that were likely the right ones for the life cycle of the business as well as his team, he hadn't addressed the elements of the transition process. By being curious and open to what was going on for people, there were a few things that were revealed. Even though he had received input into the changes, he hadn't adequately addressed the endings. As a result, his team was not embracing the new beginning and, in fact, in some ways, sabotaging it. They were living in the in-between and also holding on to what had already ended. It became apparent that many of his people had a long-standing connection not just to the brand but also to their client relationships and the way they carried out their roles.

The changes in sales territories and structure meant that client connections that had been cultivated over time would be impacted. Because many on the team had been with the organization for years, decades in some cases, they were deeply connected to the brand, even down to the logo, and thus were resistant to embrace the changes. We embarked on a process to give people the opportunity to share what they needed to grieve and let go of. We gave them the chance to articulate what they would miss about the routines and structure they had come to know. Once people were heard and processed the various endings, we invited them to share what they were looking forward to about the new structure, the new collaborative process the sales team would be part of, to share how it would support meeting increased targets and even how the new logo would serve bringing the brand more in line with current practices and industry standards. The process wasn't particularly long or complex, but it honoured all the ways the team had experienced and appreciated what was. They needed a chance to say goodbye to what had been in order to see the possibilities ahead. Once their voices were heard they were able to let go and embrace the new direction. The leader, while visionary and on point, didn't initially understand the importance of the transition process and supporting people in the uncertainty of the in-between, particularly when many on the team were legacy contributors to the old system that had served them well. Once this was addressed, the team was inspired to become part of the new beginning and could move forward with fully energy. The initiative was ultimately successful and actually forged the way for new industry models and standards beyond their particular organization.

Effective leaders understand the complexity and the psychology of transition. It is happening, whether or not we are aware of it.

APPLY IT

- What is your current jolt?
- What is the change you are being called to step into?
- Where are you at in the transition process?
- Answer the questions listed above from the Transition Model.
- What emerges when you ask the questions and relate them to attaining your desired new beginning?

It is easy to believe that change is not in your control, that the process and results are determined by others, by the organizational response, by the economy, by external factors. There are elements of change and transition for which this is true—but not for all of it. You can also get caught up in driving to the fix, rushing the outcome because you are the leader, since you think the team and the organization are counting on you to get there and get there now. Or in your personal life you may want to rush to the solution because of the role you play and the responsibilities you feel with respect to the change. The truth is that change is hard. This is your life, and you can decide how you want to show up for it. The model offered here provides a way of approaching and moving through the change that optimizes choice, mindset, and direction to increase your chance of attaining a new beginning that is aligned with what you want and what is possible.

COMMIT TO IT

TAKE ON
THE TRANSITION

- What are the implications of the change and subsequent transition process you are experiencing?
- What do you need to let go of and how will you remain patient as you move toward your new beginning?
- How will you embrace the process and set yourself, others and the situation up for success?
- How will you use the model and questions to guide your thinking and actions as you take on the transition?

Will you or won't you take on and navigate the transition?

SECTION C

The Process

*"The curious paradox is that when I accept
myself just as I am, then I can change."*
Carl Rogers

We now have a common language and understanding around the foundation of this kind of development work:

- The importance of awareness as the first step.
- The power and possibility of connecting with who we are at our best.
- Embracing the reality that we are all imperfect. The more we can identify with and be "in relationship" with all parts of ourselves the more able we will be to become even better.
- Understanding the concept of mindset and that we can choose how to view things. It isn't what we see or what we experience, but how we see those things that impacts what is possible.

And Just Like That, we need to respond to life jolts. We are required to change and enter into the transition process at various points in life, in response to many kinds of challenges and opportunities.

When that jolt happens or is initiated, what comes next? It is time to customize your template for change, and to cultivate the next best version of yourself. And Just Like That, the answers will emerge.

Set yourself up for success by committing to a routine, scheduling some thinking time, and recording your thoughts.

We talked at the beginning about how you like to capture and record your thinking and your work in terms of your growth and learning. How you do this becomes even more important as you customize your process. As you enter into this phase of being a researcher in your own life, it is vital to be intentional and to both open the actual or metaphorical file and commit to a structure or a routine around it. When you schedule something, you have a better chance of getting it done.

Capture everything:
- Thoughts
- Responses
- Feelings
- Conversations
- Experiences
- Input you receive
- Information
- Momentary flashes from what you see, hear and experience
- Aha moments from all of the above

What will your routine be?
- When will you do this work?
- Where will you do this work?
- What is the best time of day or week—is it in your calendar?
- The more intentional you can be the better

Cultivating a routine around this process will serve you and increase your chance of success! Motivation or necessity may be the starting points but habits surrounding the work will sustain it.

It is time to customize a process for yourself.

Will you, or won't you?

CHAPTER 7

Cultivate Relationships

"Everything in leadership and life is about relationships."
Karen Burrows McKnight

"Choose people who lift you up."
"When they go low, we go high."
Michelle Obama

We are not meant to do this life alone.

Understanding the importance and implications of relationships is key to increasing the chance of success in facing life jolts and using them to become even better.

Life is all about relationships, and the fact is, people mess them up, damage them or create toxicity if they don't attend to them. Without healthy relationships, life challenges can take over and gather momentum of their own, leaving us feeling out of control. Cultivating relationships, with ourselves, with others and with the situation has the power to increase the chance of working through the complexity of the jolts.

If we aren't intentional about our relationships, they won't serve us or our reality. Similarly, if we don't understand the components, complexities and implications of how we show up in our relationships and what we need from them, we can't think, act or feel in ways that are beneficial. Again, the concept of awareness is critical here.

If this concept isn't embraced, it will be difficult to move to the next level of development. Remember that the balcony view in terms of evolution of self is about being "in relationship" with yourself. This objective lens is also required to view the challenge or jolt in a way that reveals possibilities. The relational vantage point will enable you to see patterns—those that support and those that get in the way.

To be effective and healthy, relationships require continuous checking in, honesty, courage, understanding and realistic expectations. These elements need to be attended to even if, and perhaps especially if there isn't agreement or alignment. This is particularly true in relationships either at work or in our personal lives when you are required to interact with others whose values or opinions are different from your own. You need to curate win-win solutions through planned approaches and conversations without deferring to anger, judgment or defensiveness. It can require being the "bigger person" which in the end is actually empowering. These same principles apply to effectively approaching the specific content of any situation faced to be able to be "in relationship" with it and thus able to move toward resolution.

You need to authentically assess what is happening in all your relationships and then be intentional about your approach. Say what you mean, ask for what you want. Clarify what others are saying and ask for feedback. Be open to what you hear. State your message in an effective, supportive way. Sharing what is really going on for you is fundamental and requires thoughtfulness and planning. The dynamic nature of relationships means this needs to be a process that you are always actively engaged in. You also need to cultivate new ideas and ways of thinking to face any new challenge in creative ways and thus achieve aligned results. You can't fully enter into the response process without interacting effectively in all the relationships connected to the challenge.

Life and leadership, at work or in your personal life, are all about how you relate. Becoming aware of your patterns and communication style as well as recognizing how you want to show up and how you actually show up are essential considerations.

It is important to become aware of your intentions in your relationships and also how they are actually received by others. This requires practice and comfort with things like boundary setting, giving, receiving, sharing, thinking, communication, authenticity, reciprocity, appropriate vulnerability, courage, and openness. Communicating and focusing on these elements create the building blocks of healthier and mutually beneficial relationships. Having the courage to ask about and uncover things unspoken, to bring them to the surface, is also essential. It is helpful to become aware of the polarities and continuums that exist between people and where your views land. Remain open, not judgmental. Owning who you are and how you are showing up in your relationships (with self, others and the situation) is the precondition for showing up even better. Attention to engaging more fully supports the creation of constructive relationships and outcomes. The goal is to align with the present, what is really happening and connect with what you want so that you increase your chance of success in getting there.

Since our lives are rooted in relationships, we need to consider how we are cultivating them. What's working for you in your relationships? What do you think would be even better?

Relationships must be worked on and built to be successful. They are key to navigating life, particularly when engaged in a transition time. Knowing who you want and need on your team during this particular time is vital. This includes who you need to be for yourself and the ideal people you need around you, whether you already have that network to tap into or whether you need to find it.

- What needs to be adjusted or paid attention to differently in terms of your relationships to support you?
- What do you need more or less of?
- How are you ensuring effective and productive communication?
- In what ways could you proactively nurture your relationships?

CONNECT IT

There are many examples from workplace and leadership perspectives when it comes to highlighting the importance of relationships. Think about when you enter a new role—you are meeting your colleagues for the first time and as the newbie you are figuring out how to develop relationships and who you want to connect with, while at the same time assessing the existing team relationships. Establishing connections with others is an essential and fundamental piece of the initial fit in a new organization or role and is directly related to achieving early success.

Another key example that highlights the importance of relationships is watching how a leader merges cultures after an acquisition. I have been inspired working with leaders doing an effective job, and also called in to support leaders who were struggling with the complexities of this task. The leader who focuses on talking to and hearing from people at all levels of both organizations is better poised to create alignment with the merged teams. One leader I worked with spent the first quarter post-acquisition personally conducting focus groups, meeting individually with people, and creating themed business and social experiences for the two cultures to meet, share and interact. Understanding, respecting and cultivating relationships is key. Successfully leading the creation of a new culture involves paying attention to all of the relationships—those on the team of the company being acquired, as well as their relationship to the structures and systems of the company they are joining. It is also important to sensitively bring together the new teams in the merged culture. Acknowledging "what was" in terms of relationship structures in both organizations matters. Then, intentionally facilitating conversations to identify goals, clarify roles and establish new rules of engagement will inspire people to engage because they feel involved in the process. Operationalizing the new structure strategy plan, when based on healthy interpersonal connections, is more likely to succeed. It is the people who bring the plan to life, regardless of what the numbers say. Taking the time, even in the craziness of the acquisition logistics, to respect what has worked for people, adequately allowing people to articulate and let go of their previous association to their role, their team, and their organization enables the creation of new relationships that will benefit the emerging culture.

Where do I even begin to give examples in terms of personal life? Every time you face a challenge the place to start is with your relationships. Firstly, you have to ensure that you are grounded in your strengths and ready to move forward and lead your life. Then you need to do an external scan—who's on your team? Who do you need on your team? Who do you need to meet to invite onto your team? Whose presence do you need to put boundaries around? This is about shining the light on the nature and quality of your relationships to ensure you've got what you need. Who's on your "committee" for the life events you are navigating?

All the positive ones like graduations, weddings, promotions, retirements, christenings, birthdays, holiday celebrations and vacations.

And all the difficult ones like illness, addiction, death, accidents, financial hardship, divorce or job loss.

Play out the movie of each of these situations—if you are the main character, who are your supporting cast members and extras—your people? Who would you call? If you don't have someone to call, how can you cultivate relationships to gain that support?

We are not meant to navigate life alone, but we always have to start with ourselves—the only person we actually have control over, even though we often wish it were otherwise. It is about awareness and acceptance, but also about being in a relationship with yourself—a key tenet of self-development.

As you explore the relationship with yourself, you come to realize that there is a delicate balance between accepting who you are at the core and having the courage to make shifts that you come to realize may serve you better. Identifying what your values are, what you stand for, what you want, your strengths, as well as all the things that get in your way, such as your inner critic and your imperfections enable you to evolve. Embrace all of yourself, including the quirks, the inner rebel and all the positive qualities that have enabled you to thrive. Use all of it as a springboard for moving toward who you want to become. It is the totality that makes you who you are.

We are required to show up differently in each relationship in our lives while remaining true to our essence. Awareness about what works is key to becoming our best and navigating our lives and work in a way that aligns with happiness and the ideal. We need to be solid, consistent, aware and intentional about these relationships and know what supports us and others as well as what gets in the way or what is hampering successful outcomes.

Unconditionally accepting yourself, especially during challenging or transitional times, is vital because these are precisely the times the inner critic is trying to "get in", talk louder and impact more powerfully. You need to counter this by cultivating a positive relationship with yourself. It is about connecting with the unique and specific things that come together to make you "you". Your individual brand as a person and a leader. I think about the "get dressed for the day" metaphor that was passed down from my grandmother to my mother and then to me and my siblings...choose what is appropriate to put on for the day and its events and before you head out the door take one last look at yourself. Take in who you are and how you will show up fully and confidently and then forget about yourself so you can truly be present for others and what you are being called to do—powerful and empowering.

APPLY IT

Successful people understand that habits and rituals serve their relationship with self, others and the world. Well-grounded leaders engage regularly in practices to ensure they touch base with themselves first so they can go out into their day well-equipped, wherever it might take them, ready to fully engage. Many people I work with are focused on being there for others and thus there is resistance to taking time for self care. In fact, there is often a belief that it is selfish. To challenge this, I would like to introduce the concept of "self full". Taking time for yourself actually fills you and enables you to be there for others even more! Viewing it in this way helps give permission for something I believe is a requirement for servant leadership whether at work or in your personal life.

What is your practice? What are your routines?

Developing Your Personal Routine

My suggestion is to customize a routine that works for you and ensure you do it regularly over time until it becomes a habit. Then take time to connect the dots in terms of how you feel when you commit and follow through. As with all of my recommendations, making it fit you and your life is vital.

Here are some of my guidelines for creating your practice. Note that it doesn't exclusively need to be a morning routine if that doesn't fit for you. It could be weekly, nightly, at midday, on weekends or at some other regular time entirely. The point is to create habits and rituals that work to ground you and take you into a focused place that sets you up to connect with yourself, others and situations. These established routines are called "practices" for a reason. You need to repeat what works for you for them to enhance who you are becoming.

Think about learning to play an instrument or a sport. Initially, there is a need to be laser focused on the theory and the specifics. You start out very deliberately, one note or skill at a time. With practice you begin to be able to string the elements together with less effort and, over time, it becomes natural and seamless. With continued practice you are able to get into the flow of the activity. Note that without regular engagement the skills won't be sustained or improved. The same is true for establishing personal routines supporting your development.

These potential ideas and resources are for your consideration to cultivate your routine. Many successful leaders and people who experience deep happiness (from an internal world standpoint) attribute it to their daily morning rituals. The most effective rituals are customized, and they set the tone for the day. They re-energize, build focus and eliminate stress. The key is to have them become part of your life—something you look forward to as a way to ground yourself before setting out to accomplish all the tasks and responsibilities of daily work and life. Personal rituals help set intentions and increase the chance you will show up in the world the way you want.

Considerations include:

- An intentional space—comfort, symbols, atmosphere, ambience.
- An invocation—a reflective "checking in", a few deep breaths, prayer for those who resonate with this practice, listening to a piece of music—something to call and connect with the frame of mind to be open and receptive to the experience and learning.
- A mindfulness practice—for instance, breathing, a brief meditation or an affirmation.
- An input piece—such as reading some inspirational quotes, a chapter of a book, listening to a podcast or song, reading a poem, watching a TED talk.
- A reflection—journaling or intentionally reflecting on the input you are gathering or on your current goal. Delve into the life question you are exploring. Set daily intentions based on your present state of being. Write thoughts and insights connected to your desired "future self", or have an internal conversation.
- Physical exercise—it can range from a few minutes of stretching to a full-on workout—whatever fits for you and "wakes up" your system connecting you to your physical presence.
- A way of moving into the reality of the day—read the news, make your daily to-do list, go through emails that have accumulated, or healthy meal planning.
- Then start the day!

This is about creating a symbiotic reciprocal relationship with yourself. If you do that you will know what that is like and thus be able to replicate it with others.

Next, move into the realm of relationship with others. They say it takes a village—who is in yours and what are the nature and quality of the relationships within it? How do they complement and encourage your goals and purpose? What intention do you bring to your relationships with others?

Think about the concentric circles of relationships—starting close, immediate family, friends, colleagues and then work your way out. How do you bring your authentic self to your various relationships?

In the different spheres of your life—what are the templates and boundaries around your relationships? How do they create the optimal win-win? How do you and can you show up differently in relationships depending on the context? Focus on what positive interactions, behaviour, presence and encouragement would look like. When you prepare to go into a meeting or a function check in with yourself. Set specific intentions about how you want to show up. Think through who you want to connect with, what questions you want to ask and what conversations are important for the specific scenario.

Physicist David Bohm's concept of dialogue is supportive when thinking about how to foster authentic, mutually beneficial communication. He believes that if people understand the true nature of dialogue and commit to it, solutions for all human misalignments can be found—everything from personal disagreements to world peace. Each participant needs to approach an interaction committed to the true spirit of dialogue. This includes being clear on your own thoughts without being overly wedded to them and being genuinely open to hearing where others are coming from. If each person does this and is open to really listening to the perspective of others all the ideas can be put metaphorically on the table. People then can see the range of thinking, look for connections, and perhaps create even better solutions or relationships—between individuals and ideas. Pre-planning and establishing rules of engagement increase the chance that satisfaction can be achieved.

It is interesting that some relationships don't even have definitions that adequately convey what they represent. Think about how you view the range of relationships you have—from the peripheral acquaintance, the person at Starbucks who makes your coffee each day, to your most intimate connections. It isn't the definition of the relationship that determines the impact but rather what it means to you—how it inspires, energizes, informs and enables you to be your best and how you, in turn, do the same for the other person. Your constellation and what makes it up is yours alone. We are fed and able to function optimally when we cultivate our "tribe". This is the group of relationships, and the varied kinds of connections that enable us to be truly seen, heard and feel most alive.

Some titles don't describe the power, from an empowerment standpoint, or impact of a relationship. A colleague can be a peer—or a mentor—or a true friend—or maybe all three. A relative can be in title only or the connection developed and cultivated can bring that to life in a different and deeper way. You can be a boss or a leader. You can be a friend or confidante, sibling or "soul sister", neighbour or friend. There are different connotations based on titles but also based on our experience in the actual way each person shows up in the relationship and thus the meaning made from the unique and specific connection. As trust is cultivated and reciprocity evolves relationships deepen... or we decide that keeping a relationship at surface-level suits us just fine.

Sometimes boundaries in relationships need to be changed—or they change because of circumstances. Someone getting a promotion may require a new and different relationship with co-workers. Or a divorce might mean that a family relationship takes on an alternative form. There needs to be intention brought to these shifts to ensure healthy new relationships or a new next iteration of the relationship is created. You need to be able to bring your evolving authentic self to the relationship. It is important to be reality based, present and realistic about what's possible. Sometimes it requires painful changes. It is about the importance of attending to what's working, what isn't, and what would make it even better.

You need to have a realistic and honest connection with not only your intention in how you want to interact with others and the world but also an understanding of whether or not the actual impact of how you show up aligns with that intention. Are there gaps between these? What do others see, feel and experience in their relationship with you? Think back to the multiple perspectives awareness exercise, and what people notice about you when you are at your best and alternatively, when you aren't at your best.

What kind of relationships do you currently have and what would be your ideal? It is easy for time to go by and let relationships drift apart. How do you make the effort to connect regardless of how busy you are? What are the practical and intentional ways you tend to relationships in any given week? Gary Chapman's five love languages highlight that we not only need to communicate regularly, but also to do so in a way that works for others to feel fully seen and heard. He describes the different preferences as words of affirmation, quality time, receiving gifts, acts of service and physical touch. Taking the time to consider what you need and what others require can help you plan the specifics of how you foster your connection with others. While these languages need to be adapted appropriately depending on the nature of the relationship, these lenses can be useful in personal life and work.

Consider the elements of relationships and how you are showing up in terms of:

- Communication
- Caring
- Respect
- Boundaries
- Trust
- Reciprocity
- Interactions, activities and time

Bringing intention and skill (which can be learned) to all facets of your relationships will increase your chance of receiving and giving the support needed on this crazy journey through life. The relationship principles also apply to the situations you face. Being open, honest, responsive and in a reciprocal relationship with your current reality supports the process of resolution versus being reactive or letting the situation control you.

Intentional Conversations

Effective communication is the key to healthy relationships. How do you prepare for achieving the outcomes you want and that also work for others? Planning your conversations, especially the difficult ones, can be aided by pre-planning and intention. The template below offers a process to do this. Try it and notice the impact, especially when you are wanting and needing support in terms of navigating a challenge or transition.

Intentional Conversation Template

Positioning and Preparation

- How do you want to "show up" in the conversation?
- What works for you in terms of being grounded and prepared intellectually, physically and emotionally?
- What facts and information do you need to gather?
- Who, if anyone, do you need to consult?
- How can you play out the "movie in your mind" in terms of the possible outcomes?

Delivery Planning

- What is the "outline" for the conversation and what is the appropriate time and place?
- How do you want to deliver the message and what do you want and need to say?
- How will you deliver the message in a way that creates possibility and movement forward?

Dialogue

- How will you ensure you are open to reciprocity in the conversation, being open to hearing and taking in the other person's perspective on the issue?
- What questions do you want or need to ask to ensure you understand other possible viewpoints?
- How will the other person know you are interested in hearing where they are coming from and what their perspective is?

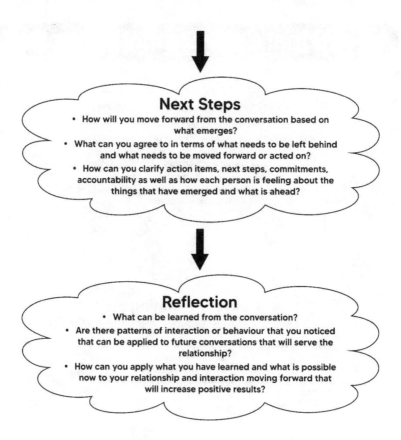

Once we are grounded in how we want our relationship with ourselves and with others to be, we can approach them from an empowered and supportive perspective.

There can be resistance to the idea that actively working on relationships can have a positive impact. It is easy to think I am who I am so take me as I am. Some default to the position that if a relationship isn't working, the answer is to let it go; or that feeling out of sync with either yourself or others is just a part of life that has to be accepted. You might be thinking that your relationships have worked—and if not you accepted the shifts that evolved. You have enjoyed success to date, so why do you need to think about relationships or change them? If it isn't broken it doesn't need to be fixed. You might even think that your job as a leader is to lead and the job of others is to follow, particularly during times of crisis or change. During challenging times, leaders can revert back to command-and-control styles versus embracing servant leader relationship skills. You might even be unclear about what the concept of relationship with self means. Connecting with these ideas makes all the difference when setting out to successfully meet a change or challenge in life and work.

To ensure readiness for navigating a jolt, it is critical to lay the relationship foundations, including:

- Having a realistic understanding of the relationships you currently have—with self, others and the situation—and acknowledging the range of relationships that support and serve you.
- Making a commitment to cultivate better, more effective relationships on all levels.
- Recognizing that for now you may need to develop different relationship boundaries.
- Taking a step back from some relationships and even creating and cultivating new ones for this part of your journey supports the process.

COMMIT TO IT

CULTIVATE RELATIONSHIPS

- What resonates in terms of your relationships with yourself, others and your situation?
- What personal routines can you create to support yourself?
- What are the ways you can attend to the elements of healthy relationships to increase your chance of success in navigating your current reality?
- How can you be more intentional about planning your conversations and communication?
- Who do you need on your team and what can you do to cultivate the best fit relationships you will benefit from?

Will you or won't you take action to cultivate your relationships?

CHAPTER 8

Seek and Gather Input

"Curiosity is an act of vulnerability and courage. We need to be brave enough to want to know more."
Brené Brown

When we experience or initiate a jolt or add a new variable, our life equation is about to change. This requires new ways of thinking and acting—we don't know what we don't know.

What we knew to be true—our patterns, responses, routines—no longer fit once the new variable is introduced. Things no longer work, even if we wish it wasn't so. Input is required to face the new reality and create a new normal that aligns at this particular point in life.

If you resist this, you will be dealing with facing the jolt or challenge with the same responses that have become your go-to patterns. The definition of insanity is doing the same thing over and over and hoping for a different outcome. You can't learn, grow or get to the next level by staying where you are or in your comfort zone. If you are stagnant or stuck, you can't become the next best version of yourself. Vicious cycles are created when one negative thing feeds off another and creates an inertia spiralling downward. What is needed is the creation of the opposite—as each positive element is created the spiral spins upward creating a momentum that gains ground and substance as it rises—sometimes described as a virtuous cycle.

This information-gathering stage in the process is about being curious about where to look to approach, and ultimately solve, the current challenge. The focus here is facing the reality with intention and a curious, open mindset without rushing to solution.

Ask yourself what input is required to face and successfully navigate this particular issue? When a variable changes, you enter into uncharted waters and may be filled with the uncertainty that comes with that. The growth mindset is key.

When a variable changes as a result of facing or initiating a jolt, you need to enter into investigation mode. You will benefit from becoming a researcher in your own life. What do you need to learn? What do you need to find out that is relevant to your situation? What do you need to read? What questions are arising? Who do you need to reach out and talk to? Who has navigated a similar challenge? What do you need to watch or listen to? What information is available on the theme that relates to your specific reality?

This research stage requires a lot of patience, as referenced in the transition model. Especially for smart, successful people who have typically always achieved what they set out to accomplish, there is a tendency to want to find a solution immediately. It is important, however, if you find yourself becoming impatient, try to stay in data collection mode without prematurely trying to land on the answer. Follow and trust the process.

At the beginning of this section, I invited you to consider and decide how you would capture or record this process. As you move into the data collection phase, it is vital that you compile information from your conversations, reading, podcasts, thinking and questions and record the relevant findings in such a way that can be easily referenced later. Some ideas for sources that can be tapped into include the following:

- Google your topic or theme—being careful to check sources and not believe everything you read!
- Connect with people who have walked this path before you
- Create coffee chat lists—who can you talk to about this?
- Access offerings from people with experience in this area—books, articles, podcasts, videos, courses
- Reach out to groups and associations
- Connect with colleagues and other professionals
- Research online communities

View everything with an open mindset. Seek to understand the landscape of your particular situation and the range of possible responses. Remain curious. Keep asking "what else"?

Be open to a variety of resources for your research. Some people are readers, some listeners, some talkers. Others are watchers, hands-on doers, creators. Get to know your preferences as well as being open to expanding your comfort zone by employing different modalities.

CONNECT IT

There are many examples of businesses that have succeeded in getting the input required when facing a crossroads. There are equally well-known businesses that didn't get out in front of what was ahead for them and gather the data that could have served them. Netflix is in the former category, Blockbuster in the latter. What kind of thinking and research did Netflix do to have the foresight to think that bringing movies, entertainment and shows directly to the consumer would be the future? Think about their initial offering that started with a DVD arriving in the mailbox, eventually evolving into what we have today where almost anything can be streamed any time from any number of devices in the home! Compare that to Blockbuster, which stayed committed to their model. While their business structure helped them achieve an incredible degree of success for a time, they didn't open up their thinking and innovate as was required to stay relevant in a changing global market. Hence, they no longer exist.

We've each had to chart our own career path. This is an excellent example of knowing that you need to go out into the world and learn more, connect with, and meet new people; apply your skills, experience and credentials in new ways; create a map of connections; clarify your vision; and enlist the expertise of others in order to chart a course that fully aligns with what you want. This is particularly critical in these times of exponential change. Inform yourself and stay ahead of the curve by reaching out to friends, role models, mentors, formal networking groups or a career coach. Use a career-pathing template to gain input. Utilize brainstorming, podcasts, books and industry journels—immerse yourself in all things related to your next best career fit. We have all lived this example when we go all in to seek and gather the input required for the next best chapter in our career. These steps can be replicated and applied to whatever situation is being navigated.

APPLY IT

Pattern Recognition Exercise

Revisit the Review Your Jolts exercise. What patterns have worked for you in the past that you can apply now? What things did you do to navigate past jolts? How can you use the template you created to help frame this input gathering stage?

The task here is to view what you have already lived in a new way—looking at it from a research and curiosity perspective in service of articulating the patterns that work for you. Then you can apply them to the situation you are in now.

Have the courage to stay in the process. When I did this exercise, I was informed and reminded by my past experience to trust the process. This is the part when you go back up onto the balcony and look down. You look for the connection between things and what might fit for you currently.

Perspective Wheel Exercise

It is easy to get stuck in viewing a challenge from one perspective. As you engage in the research phase it is helpful to generate alternative perspectives. The Perspective Wheel Exercise supports a growth mindset and can reveal different ways of approaching things.

Generating Alternative Perspectives

Current Perspective

- Think about other possible perspectives
- Keep asking "what else?" until all sections are filled
- What do you notice?

What are all the possible ways of seeing the issue you face? What are the components? Start with the reality of how you are viewing the situation in one segment on the wheel. Then brainstorm all the other ways you might view the situation. Play with opposites, positives and negatives, possible views from your vantage point and then from that of others. Be curious about the various potential and additional elements connected to the issue. Note the things that don't initially come to mind for you.

Think about what aligns immediately and then reach for ideas that at first glance don't appear to fit at all. There are always a variety of perspectives connected to any challenge even if not apparent at first. Force crazy outside-the-box thinking. Again, keep asking "what else"?

Once you have generated multiple perspectives take a step back, look at all the ideas and ask yourself:

- What do you notice?
- What resonates with you?
- What surprises you?
- What would you like to learn more about?
- Where are you drawn to focus?
- Which perspectives intrigue you?
- Which perspectives do you know don't fit for you?

This exercise can guide your thinking in new ways. This broadens your thinking and expands the possibilities of what input you might gather.

Revisit Previous Exercises

All of the preceding parts of the book come into play during this research and input phase. How do all of these aspects impact the possible approaches you could take and what you want and need to learn?

The input you gather, and the possible new perspectives can cause paradigm shifts.

Note your energy points during this process—what inspires you and what drains you?

Overlay the foundational pieces—awareness, best self, imperfections, mindset. What is going on as you consider what the work stands on?

Be honest about the life equation variables that have changed and what the current jolt represents. Understand the transition process and set yourself up for success in your relationships so you can do the research and gather the input that would serve you and your situation.

- Where are you getting tripped up?
- What do you want to pursue?
- How do you overlay and apply the preceding information and ideas?
- How does it all work together when you intentionally step into the research?
- What other learning would serve you?
- What rises to the top?
- What are the new variables and how do they come together to form the new question you are stepping into or creating?

You might be thinking that there often isn't time to research or gather data, that the issue is too pressing to stop and take this time. Or you might not know where to begin or where to look. You may also think that the circumstances just are what they are and that you don't have any control. The reality is that you can't afford not to spend time in this phase—this is the in-between as discussed in the transition model and attending to it will expand your capacity. Empower yourself and increase your chance of alignment, success and creating the next best version of yourself by stepping into it fully—it works!

COMMIT TO IT

SEEK AND GATHER INPUT

- What do you need to learn to better equip yourself to address your current situation, and where can you look?
- What alternative perspectives can you generate to broaden your view of your situation?
- What works for you when seeking information? (reading, talking, writing, watching, listening ...)
- How will you stay curious, open and resist attaching what you find to solutions prematurely?
- How will you capture the data so you can assess it once you have fully explored?

Will you or won't you seek and gather the input you would benefit from?

CHAPTER 9

Experiment

"It is not that I'm so smart.
But I stay with the questions much longer."
Albert Einstein

Once you have gathered the information, it is time to apply it and experiment. This part of the process brings ideas to life by trying out potential solutions.

When you know one situation, you know one situation. All that you have gathered, thought about, received support for and learned needs to be tested so the aligned solution unfolds. It isn't direct drive from the jolt to the solution—remember that the tendency is to think something new begins when something ends which isn't the whole story. You need to really step into what is before you, live the in-between and bring the ideas to life by trying them on to see if they fit. This is the work of solving the equation.

Without taking the time for the experimentation stage you will waste time, energy and get caught up in the momentum of the vicious cycle. You can get wedded to your initial "solve" and invest in it, without being sure that it aligns with what you want. You will avoid taking the next steps or you can get caught up in action that may not meet your goal. You will also be vulnerable in terms of staying within your comfort zone and not growing, changing, evolving and thus being able to take the next step toward becoming even better.

Once you have gathered the data and cast the net widely in terms of all the possibilities related to the issue you need to funnel it down to the key things that need addressing and then experiment. This is the action part of the process that spurs growth. As you experiment pay attention to your motivation to:

- Try new things
- Think differently
- Act differently
- Sense differently
- Feel differently

Of all the things you have thought about in relation to the jolt how do you prioritize the information you have gathered? What is a place to start? What is one step forward?

- What about all of this really matters to you?
- What is the most important thing that needs to be addressed?
- What is bothering you the most?
- What do you need to plan?
- Of the things you want to try
    - How is it going to work?
    - How does or might it fit:

- into your personal life and routines?
- into your family life?
- with your team?
- in your organization?

CONNECT IT

There are many organizations that have gathered the courage to step out on a limb, experiment and to try new things. Who would have thought that by pressing an app on your phone your Uber would arrive and take you to your destination? It was an innovative concept and one that the industry most poised to experiment with resisted—the taxi industry. Or what about the companies that initially experimented with online grocery orders? Innovative organizations had to have the courage to experiment with different ways of doing things based on creative thinking, research, conversations and data gathering. These are the organizations that have become industry leaders. They are the ones who stood bravely on the edge of their sector looking forward and moving outward. Through trial and error, they creatively forged completely different ways of doing business that have now become the norm.

Think about getting ahead on your retirement plan or someone you know who is getting ahead on their retirement plan. This notion is the gold standard for the experimentation and action phase of creating the ideal vision. These are the people who take up new hobbies, connect in new ways with their passions, learn new skills, volunteer at community organizations or dabble in the activities that they think they might be interested in before they actually find themselves in the situation. These are the role models for active experimentation. Taking hold of your vision and dipping your toes in the water, planning and then experimenting while paying attention to how things feel assures the best chance that the "what's next?" will actually work for you.

As you sift through your research, it is important to keep in mind not only the goals that have emerged But also how you will feel when you achieve them.

- How will you experiment and put together a plan based on what you have learned?
- What do you actually need or want to try?
- Who do you want to be?
- Who do you need to engage with?
- Who are the people connected to the issue or challenge who can support you?
- Who do you need to be cautious of boundaries with?
- Where is your energy and where do you want or need it to be?
- What activities fill your energy?
- What can you try out that may be connected to possible solutions and what you want?
- How are going to track your progress?

It can be helpful to think about the concept of a pilot project. It isn't about getting it right immediately. It isn't about perfection. It is about progress and process. You can always create a reason for a fresh start, to try something new or go in a different direction.

This is about consciously getting out of the fight, flight or freeze states—the vicious cycle—and beginning to create the virtuous cycle. It is about stepping into the creative thinking state where you gain momentum and move toward what you want, based on what you have learned, what you have been curious about, what you have had the courage to face and what you have prioritized.

APPLY IT

Funnelling Process

Visualizing the funnelling process is useful. This starts with going out into the world to do your research and gather your data as described in the previous chapter. You have identified and approached your research sources. Now you need to distill and prioritize the data gathered and funnel the information down to the key elements. You then take those key points back out into the world with openness and curiosity and funnel it down again. This process is repeated until you land on the most important things. Try to cull the information to the top three points that resonate.

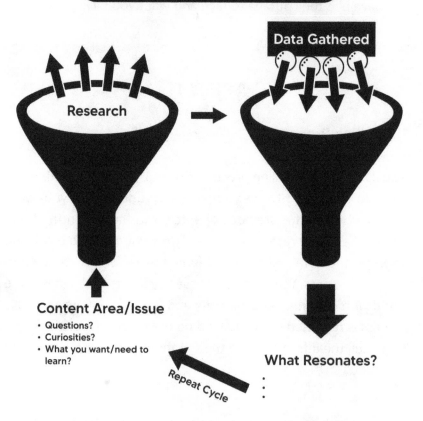

Once you have gathered the data the funnelling process hones in on the few things you can experiment with. Often this comes easily when you ask yourself which things rise to the top. You can also apply simple metrics such as rating the ideas on a scale of 1—5, based on your motivation to try them.

Prioritizing Tool

To further analyze where to begin your action and experimentation process, you can use the following tool. The goal is to try things that will have the highest impact result using the lowest effort energy. When activating the kinds of energy that fuel you less effort is required. You can look at how the possibilities you are considering land in the quadrants related to the kind of energy that would be necessary. This helps determine if the result would be ineffective, have some potential, be effective or, in the best-case scenario, ideal.

Time gets in the way, particularly when issues have to be solved immediately. Occasionally timing and circumstances are dictated and controlled by our environment or by others. While this may be true for some elements of a challenge, it is never true for all of it. Focus on what is in your control, even if it is only your mindset and have the courage to try different things.

COMMIT TO IT

EXPERIMENT

- Given what you want and the knowledge you have gained, what does ideal look like?
- Based on the information gathered and funnelling the data into the most important elements, what can you try?
- Are you willing to undertake new and different actions and thinking based on what is most relevant?
- What pilot projects will you prioritize that will have the biggest impact? Now tackle them!

Will you or won't you experiment to learn more about what fits?

CHAPTER 10

Reflect

---

*"We do not learn from experience.
We learn from reflecting on experience."*
John Dewey

*"The least of things with a meaning is worth more in life
than the greatest of things without it."*
Carl Jung

Step into it. Have the courage to really see, hear and take in what you have spent so much time learning and trying based on any particular jolt. Without identifying the meaning for you and your unique and specific situation, you will be unable to identify or embark on your next best aligned level.

Without intentional reflection you will remain vulnerable to the challenge. There will be no connecting the dots that lead to the next best-fit steps.

The meaning-making part leads directly to the customized, specific goals to meet the jolt and move forward positively and productively.

This is about connecting to self, others and the situation in ways that best serve. Reflecting on and establishing the relevant elements that matter to you creates the vision of what ideal might look and feel like—based on your process and your particular content. Meaning-making is about identifying and embracing the themes and priorities that emerge based on what you have experimented with. This is the part where you are starting to solve the equation. You are figuratively checking your work before handing it in. You feel a sense of progress and that you are getting closer to a solution.

Reflect on the data and on the action steps you have tried. What information have you collected? Can you objectively view the various components of the challenge or situation? How will you relate to the data and what you now know? It is important to gain perspective on the individual parts as jolts are often complex. Of the things you have prioritized and experimented with what things rise to the top? What resonates or feels like it fits for you? Consider what is possible, what you want and what the ideal looks like.

Before the equation is solved, step back from it in order to see what is meaningful—reflect on possible solutions based on what you have experienced and learned to date. Any kind of meaningful growth requires a continuous action and reflection cycle. The experimentation was based on the research, the input, and the people you brought into your process. Now there needs to be reflection to make meaning from what you have learned and tried.

While you have looked at patterns, trends, preferences, strengths, ways of coping and triumphing, you have never been in this exact place before. Focus your curiosity on connecting the dots. You can't do that when you are "in it", so you need to step back to create some distance between yourself and the situation to truly reflect on it. Step outside of yourself and go back up to the balcony. There is a specific kind of reflection required, one where you stop and say, "Ok, what does all this mean to me based on what matters and how it connects to what I desire and how I want to feel"? You tried different things, you had the courage to face your emotions and your responses. Where is the potential path to your next level? What is ideal in this situation—what things have you tried that have worked, and how do you continue to build on those things to create more momentum forward?

This stage is about pulling together all the different threads and weaving the tapestry that you want to plan for next. It's about being honest and realistic about what works and what would be even better. It is also about the new perspectives gained and crafting the ideal based on all of what you now see because of how you have looked at and experienced things. This involves really taking in the connected observations and assessing how they relate to you, those around you and the larger context. This enables you to see the way forward.

When you are solving the complex math equation there is a point where you stop, examine the steps taken so far and gain an understanding of how all the variables work together. You analyze the progress in terms of how the steps are leading towards the answer for this current question or reality. You are almost there.

CONNECT IT

Leaders reflect, prioritize and discern what really matters in the annual planning and forecasting process. The most effective leaders are able to convey their strategy in the form of a one-page plan. The leader who when creating a strat plan does the required research, gets the input necessary, encourages feedback loops and then experiments with bringing different ideas to life is best able to cull those ideas and funnel them down into a one-pager that captures what will actually work for the customers, finance, operations and organizational teams. The leader who is able to consider the connection between best strategy ideas, the actions necessary to achieve them, and how the overall plan will land for all stakeholders as it rolls out, increases the chance that the plan will not only be followed but also will meet with success. Through effective reflection the essence of what has been discovered and what the premium solution looks like is crystalized. What is essential can be articulated in a format that is easy to digest and understand.

The essay writing process is a good metaphor for how we make meaning. Think about the old school way of writing a paper—you used to have to go to the library and search the general Dewey Decimal numbers for your given topic, scanning the spines of books to see which titles stood out for you. If you were like me, you then pulled the relevant books off the shelf, scanned them and decided on the eight or so books that you were going to take back to your residence room. Then you started the process of reading through them and capturing all the parts that fit with your topic. Once you had learned enough, you were able to connect all of these thoughts and distil them into a thesis statement. You made meaning from the vast array of information and you culled it down into what matters most for you in the development of your viewpoint and what you would set out to prove in the essay. You started to develop your "why we should care" about what you were going to say and how it would fit both for you and for others. This is the process you can overlay on navigating your current reality.

APPLY IT

When you go back up to the balcony and look at all that you have done, thought about, wondered about and experimented with you can see all the interactions and connections in terms of what resonates vis-à-vis your current reality. From that view how do things fit together? Consider the moments, the pain, the crisis, the joy, the successes, the vision. What is the story that you see? Storytelling is central to making meaning. What is the story you are crafting?

> *"You can't connect the dots looking forward; you can only connect them looking backwards. So you have to trust that the dots will somehow connect in your future. You have to trust in something—your gut, destiny, life, karma, whatever."*
> Steve Jobs

Stories create maps. They allow us to bring others along the path we have created, to share the way we are experiencing our life. They allow us to share our visions of the future. They allow us to share our dreams. They allow us to make the complex understandable. They allow us to inspire. They allow us to create change. Stories allow us to move forward.

Essentially, a story expresses how and why life changes. It begins with a situation in which life is relatively calm but then there's an event. In writing it is called the inciting incident and it throws the main character's life out of the balance they previously enjoyed up until that disruption. It could be any number of things such as a new job, someone getting ill, or a big customer threatening to leave. The story goes on to describe how, in an effort to restore balance, the character attempts to plan responses and actions that will adequately meet the challenge before them. A good storyteller describes what it's like to deal with the opposing forces present. The most compelling writers create characters who have to dig deep, work with scarce resources, make difficult decisions, take action despite risks and ultimately discover their truth. Impactful stories provide a framework to comprehend the process of effectively moving through reality even when we experience curves or roadblocks.

Joseph Campbell, professor and author, identified common patterns that exist in narratives and mythology. People relate to the stages he calls the "Hero's Journey". His model articulates how the central character in a story is invited or compelled to go on some kind of adventure, face adversity, encounter mentors, cultivate hope, triumph over the challenge and eventually return "home" transformed. There is comfort in understanding this cycle. It can normalize the reality that the trials and tribulations encountered in our own evolving life stories are part of the transformation process.

Since there is clearly no recipe for navigating complexity, we can learn from each other by creating and sharing our stories. Thinking through what you have learned in this particular situation in a story format can help uncover meaning.

- Frame your story—what is the context?
- What was your initial outlook and approach?
    - What was the original plan?
    - What resources did you seek—who did you involve?
    - Trigger your memory in terms of the details and steps
- As you rolled out your plan—what were the challenges—how did you have to change plans "en route"?
- How was the process and progress for you—the ups and downs, the things you had to consider and reflect on?
- What were the turning points, setbacks and complications?
- What new decisions did you make?
- What was the final push or what do you anticipate will be the final push?
- What was the outcome or transformation, or if you aren't there yet then what is your hope?
- What enabled or might enable the successful outcome in spite of the complex nature of the situation?
- What elements did you tap into to be in the frame of mind to be creative and "solve" through the complexity?

As you "write" the story you are currently immersed in, how is it moving toward a transformative ending? How might it?

The truth is you can't force learning or meaning. It evolves from the process. Some things happen and it can take years to be able to look back and gain the meaning. It requires belief and hope to stay patient through the process. Things don't happen to us, they just happen. You can be the author of the response and of the ultimate ending to the story.

COMMIT TO IT

REFLECT

- What kind of reflection can you do to cultivate the conditions for meaning to evolve?
- Of everything you are learning and trying what resonates for you?
- What story are you writing based on all that you have discovered?
- How are you going to plan for and create the desired ending to the story?

Will you or won't you reflect and make meaning from your current process?

CHAPTER 11

The Aha—
And Just Like That—
Bring it Together

"Creativity and insight almost always involve an experience
of acute pattern recognition: the eureka moment in which
we perceive the interconnection between disparate concepts
or ideas to reveal something new."
Jason Silva

There is power in staying with the process for as long as it takes
for you. The answer and clarity will emerge from the work. It is
essential to be patient and trust the process.

As indicated earlier, And Just Like That happens in two different
ways—firstly, when the jolt hits or is initiated, and then again in
the moment when you know what to do and how to respond.

By being aware, knowing who you are at your best, by embracing
your imperfections and choosing your mindset you become ready

to take on whatever jolts life has in store for you. You can face them and enter into the transition process. Then you can customize your template through cultivating relationships, becoming a researcher in your life, experimenting and then connecting meaning to find and create the ideal in each situation. And Just Like That, you will know who you want to be, how you want to show up as well as what ideal looks like and feels like. You not only have to know where to look but also when the next level of clarity has emerged so you can move forward and solve your current equation.

The pivotal moments can be missed if you aren't paying attention. If you aren't on the developmental learning path, you decrease your chance of successfully navigating the jolt. If you aren't attuned to the process, you can miss moments of clarity—the Aha moments— and thus miss the chance to do the "next best thing" for yourself, others and the situation. Or you may pursue a solution that is not the best fit for you.

In the Merriam-Webster dictionary, the Aha moment is defined as "a moment of sudden realization, inspiration, insight, recognition or comprehension". In other words, the "eureka" moment of insight or discovery. You can't plan for or force them. Often people talk about it just coming to them randomly in the shower or when they hear a particular song lyric—it emerges when the mind is quiet and idle, even while thinking about other things. In those moments there is a connected observation, And Just Like That, it all comes together. This clarity isn't actually out of the blue. It is cultivated by what has evolved in your work, how you have focused your energy and activated your best self. It is as a result of your intention to go in and dig deep.

This is about stepping into the solved equation—the clarity, the knowing where to go, what that feels like, what the ideal actually is. And Just Like That can be an epiphany, or a series of Aha moments that culminate in a sense of knowing. It isn't the destination per se but discovering which road to take, the manner of travelling and the "practice" required to get there. Moving forward with focus, passion and clarity of vision becomes possible.

These Aha moments also come when you resist holding too tightly—when you release being overly wedded to the outcome. It isn't letting go completely but it is holding on differently so there is capacity for what resonates to reveal itself. That revelation indicates where you need to go and what you need to do to get there.

Once you have it, don't get distracted. Use the clarity to advance decisively and in service of the next best "whatever".

Oprah Winfrey says, "You can't have an Aha moment unless you already knew it. The Aha is a remembering of what you already knew, articulated in a way to resonate with your own truth." Building on that, I would add that you "know" because you have done the work, the discovering and the uncovering of the elements. This process helps you cultivate, connect with memories, remember what you want and need but also how to create new connections that fit for now. This can't be prescribed, taught or learned. It evolves. Trust and patience are required, and it doesn't need to feel like you are jumping off a cliff.

CONNECT IT

This book doesn't conclude with an ultimate final result. Rather, it ends with knowing where you want to go, who you want to be, what you want and perhaps most importantly, clarity in terms of the meaning and feelings connected with these things. This is where there is excitement in terms of moving toward the solved equation now that you know how the variables fit together and what feels genuinely right.

Think about Aha moments in business, in roles you have had, in big decisions you have worried about. Think about what it would have been like to be sitting around that boardroom table at Apple, whose core business at the time was selling computers, when somebody shared their Aha moment and tabled the question—what if we started to sell music? Can you imagine what the initial response might have been? Employees must have thought that they were in the wrong room and in the wrong meeting. Yet somebody had the courage to take all of the information gathered sort through it, experiment with possible business ideas, connect to what might be actually possible and prioritize the meaning from all those things culminating in posing the question, "What if we sold music"? Crazy but true!

From a personal standpoint, I have vivid memories of what has perhaps been the most impactful Aha moment in my life. I was lying on a gurney in a hallway at the hospital after another intervention and years of struggling with infertility. There I was, yet again, hoping that this time things would work out and I would become pregnant. I had spent a great deal of time processing, learning, connecting with people who could support me and my husband, on our journey to become parents. And without even knowing yet the outcome of this particular procedure it all came together, and it hit me. I wanted to become a parent and it didn't matter to me how that happened. This realization changed everything, and we headed into the adoption process inspired, hopeful and with a deep knowing that this was the direction that was meant to be for us and our future family. We were fully inspired and engaged. Three months later, the phone call came that we had been chosen by a birth mother and our daughter was being born two days later. It was the happiest jolt I have ever experienced! Sixteen months later, we received another call, and a third two years after that! Suffice to say that the Aha moments that emerge from dark times can lead to incredible joy, peace, gratitude and genuine happiness.

By working through this process, you are creating the conditions for your And Just Like That reality to come to fruition—your Aha moment.

The best, the ideal, the moment of truth is revealed in the Aha! Have faith—belief in self as well as in the process and when you know—recognize it, embrace it, create the plan, live the plan, step into the new beginning and enjoy living in the solved equation. This is the peak state—when everything is firing on all cylinders. Then get ready to do it again!

APPLY IT

A—Don't try to force its emergence but recognize the Aha when it reveals itself

B—Connect the Aha to a plan

C—Live the plan

The solution emerges and the Ahas evolve from the process—you will know. It is the final step in the equation, when all of a sudden it comes together, and the answer is before you.

> *"They are the accelerators of the possibilities; they dissolve boundaries and make us see things differently. Once a mind has been stretched by one Aha moment, it can never go back to its original state."*
>
> Ina Catrinescu

This is where the concept of And Just Like That comes into play again. If you have the patience, courage, vulnerability and wisdom to stay with this process your And Just Like That will guide you in what to do and where to go.

The jolt is the And Just Like That at the beginning and the Aha is the And Just Like That when you are ready for the aligned new beginning. That time of genuine thriving when you get to live for a while in the solved equation!

You now get to move toward your ideal. You stayed in the chaos long enough for clarity to emerge. Your direction reveals itself. Ambiguity is no longer felt. Instead, you see a path and one that you can not only get on but also confidently move forward on. Instead of swimming upstream you are now metaphorically in a kayak and able to navigate the rapids and move with the flow of the river in an empowered way. You feel fully immersed in the present and no longer stuck fighting against the current and all the stressful energy that requires. The focus now is on forward movement and there is renewed energy and inspiration. Excitement is generated and propels and inspires you because you are clear on your direction, and it feels right. The preoccupation and stress experienced while "figuring it out" dissipates, not just because you are hopeful that you are on the right path, but also because you can track progress and positive momentum is generated as you gain evidence each step you take toward the goal, however small. There is an effortlessness that emerges, a feeling of empowerment and a sense of calm. Actions, instead of being second-guessed, become clear. Increased performance, motivation and positivity are present and thus the "doing" doesn't feel draining—it actually feels inspiring because you know you are working toward what will work better for you, for those in your life and in terms of meeting the situation. You aren't operating from fear. There is an inner knowing that you have increased your chance of successfully handling life, where you currently are, and experiencing it fully. There is a sense of ease and hope for the future and for your ability to achieve what you have spent so much time figuring out.

Connect this to being ready to write the essay or create the one-page strat plan knowing that it feels right. It unfolds. This is what the next best version of yourself is calling for. This is your next step in terms of success.

COMMIT TO IT

THE AHA—AND JUST LIKE THAT—BRING IT TOGETHER

- What do you know for sure now?
- What clear path is before you?
- What inspired plan is possible now?
- How will you act on it?

Will you or won't you be ready to receive the Aha and step into the next best version of yourself?

THE AFTERWORD

Your New Beginning

"Do the best you can until you know better.
Then when you know better, do better."
Maya Angelou

"The most effective way to do it, is to do it."
Amelia Earhart

Think about next-level development as ascending a staircase. The great thing is that you get to bring all the previous experiences, learnings and wisdom with you at each step up. The joys, sorrows and everything in between are also part of the lived experiences that will inform and sustain you. You now have all of that as part of your internal support system and your resources to keep moving to the next level. It doesn't mean you won't be jolted again—you will—and it could even be more significant than what you have experienced previously. You will, however, be facing it with the benefit of wisdom and insight at the level you have achieved with all the resources, tools, experiences and relationships to support you. You get to overlay and bring all of it with you, to guide you, regardless of what is ahead. You can never unexperience the Aha moments.

Here is a visual of the process offered to further support you.

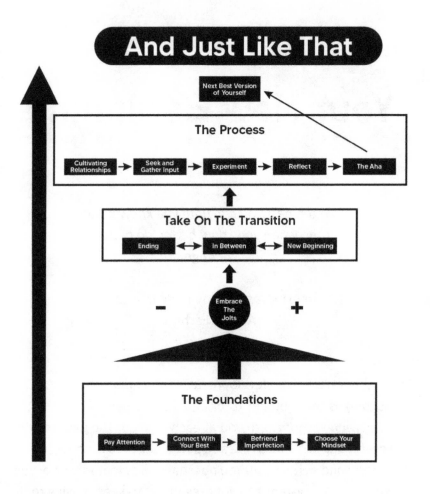

What is your path forward? The call to action is to apply what you have learned to create the next best version of yourself in leadership and life.

Now, over to you—will you, or won't you?

Notes

_____

_____

_____

_____

_____

_____

_____

_____

_____

_____

_____

_____

_____

_____

_____

Resources

Adams, Marilee G. *Change Your Questions, Change Your Life: 10 Powerful Tools for Life and Work.* Berrett-Koehler Publishers, 2009.

Bes, Fernando Trias, and Alex Rovira Celma. *Good Luck: Creating the Conditions for Success in Life and Business.* Jossey-Bass, 2004.

Bohm, David. *On Dialogue.* Edited by Lee Nichol, Routledge, 1996.

Bridges, William. *Transitions: Making Sense of Life's Changes.* 2nd ed., Da Capo Lifelong Books, 2004.

Campbell, Joseph. *The Hero with a Thousand Faces.* 2nd ed., Princeton University Press, 1972.

Chapman, Gary. *The 5 Love Languages: The Secret to Love That Lasts.* Northfield Publishing, 2010.

Dweck, Carol S. *Mindset: The New Psychology of Success.* Random House, 2006.

Gay, Ross. *The Book of Delights.* Algonquin Books, 2019.

Heifetz, Ronald A., et al. *The Practice of Adaptive Leadership: Tools and Tactics for Changing Your Organization and the World.* Harvard Business Review Press, 2009.

Joordens, Steve. "Mind Control: Managing Your Mental Health During COVID-19." Coursera. 2020, www.coursera.org/learn/manage-health-covid-19.

Kegan, Robert. *In over Our Heads: the Mental Demands of Modern Life.* Harvard University Press, 1998.

Kegan, Robert. *The Evolving Self: Problem and Process in Human Development.* Harvard University Press, 1982.

Linley, Alex. *Average to A+ - Realising Strengths in Yourself and Others*. Capp Press, 2008.

Loehr, James, and Tony Schwartz. *The Power of Full Engagement: Managing Energy, Not Time, Is the Key to High Performance and Personal Renewal*. Free Press, 2005.

"Oprah Explains 'Aha!" Moments." Performance by Oprah Winfrey, *YouTube*, Harry Connick Jr., 7 Nov. 2017, www.youtube.com/watch?v=rw9c8CSnDaU&t=1s.

Petrie, David A., and Robert Chad Swanson. "The Mental Demands of Leadership in Complex Adaptive Systems." *Healthcare Management Forum*, vol. 31, no. 5, 2018, pp. 206–213., doi:10.1177/0840470418778051.

Seligman, Martin E. P. *Authentic Happiness: Using the New Positive Psychology to Realise Your Potential for Lasting Fulfilment*. Atria Paperback, 2002.

Seligman, Martin E. P., and Mihaly Csikszentmihalyi. "Positive Psychology: An Introduction." *American Psychologist*, vol. 55, no. 1, 2000, pp. 5–14., doi: 10.1037//0003-066X.55.1.5.

Wheatley, Margaret J. *Leadership and the New Science: Discovering Order in a Chaotic World*. 3rd ed., Berrett-Koehler, 2006.

Karen Burrows McKnight

A highly sought-after Executive Coach, Karen has been coaching and consulting at the most senior levels for 20 years. She earned her Master of Education degree, specializing in the psychology of Adult Learning and Change.

In her interactive speaking events, as well as in her facilitations and written work, Karen draws upon relevant learnings from her personal life and career as a professional coach. Keynotes reflect her talent for making lasting connections and customizing her approach to provide tailored, relevant, and most importantly, actionable insights.

Keynotes:
Navigating Transitions
Mindset for Success
Optimizing Your Energy
Customized Topics

Downloadable Resources

Visit
www.Karen-McKnight.com
to access companion pieces to the book;

- Worksheets
- Templates
- Exercises
- Coaching Tips

Leadership Experiences

Karen works with senior leaders and organizational teams to create customized experiences that raise awareness, provide insight, and inspire people to think and act differently.

Executive Coaching

Karen coaches high-performance individuals in a one on one setting. Focusing on leadership development and transitions, she supports leaders in reaching organizational, career, and personal goals.

LEADERSHIP CONNECT
WITH **KAREN MCKNIGHT**

Connect with Karen at Karen-McKnight.com to design an experience for you or your team.

About the Author

Karen is a highly sought-after Executive Coach in Toronto, Ontario, where she offers executive coaching and consulting to individuals and organizations. She is a dynamic, resourceful and sharp student, known for her listening skills and ability to quickly assess and develop customized approaches to address her clients' needs. She has been coaching senior level executives and their teams for almost 20 years, supporting them in navigating change and achieving business and personal success. Karen's expertise in the psychology of transitions, her coaching skills and her teaching and facilitation experience in the adult learning field are the foundation of her work.

Karen earned her Master of Education degree from the University of Toronto, where she specialized in the psychology of Adult Learning and Change. She went on to complete her Certified Professional Coaching Designation from The Adler School of Professional Coaching. Since 2002, she has coached and consulted through her private practice, Transitions' Edge.

Always committed to the learning process, Karen is passionate about helping others develop to the best of their ability and thrive. Throughout her work and studies, she has learned that success depends on being continually engaged, motivated and inspired in work and life. She entered the coaching profession to help people develop a framework for establishing and achieving their goals and becoming their best selves. With over 30 years of management, teaching and organizational experience in a variety of environments, Karen has helped individuals, teams and organizations consistently achieve success.

Karen and her husband, Greg, are enjoying navigating the launching process with their three children who are now all in their twenties. Karen is committed to balance, which she strives to impart to all of her clients, and when not working, enjoys fitness, community volunteering and spending time with her family at the cottage in the summer and on the slopes in the winter.

Acknowledgements

- My husband, Greg:
    - For challenging and supporting me to actually write this book, instead of just thinking and talking about it.
    - For your unwavering love and support over our almost 40-year journey together. Our jolts haven't always been easy to navigate and your commitment and patience has made all the difference in me being able to create the next best version of myself in multiple ways multiple times over the years to create our ideal life! The music, adventure and fun also add so much! Thank you doesn't seem big enough to hold all that.

- My kids, Larissa, Alison and Carter, three incredible human beings—each of you is unique and special. I am so proud, grateful and blessed to be your mom. You inspire me to continue to become even better.

- My family of origin:
    - My parents, Joan and Bob, for being so remarkable at giving us the two lasting gifts parents can give their children—one is roots, the other wings. Deep gratitude and unconditional love and respect for you both.
    - Wendy and Nancy, my best friends and sisters. I feel blessed to have two sisters who are truly my best friends. It isn't lost on me that you are and will be the longest relationships in my life. Thanks for making them amazing ones!

- Chelsie, my marketing and PR Consultant extraordinaire! I couldn't have done this without your support, expertise, patience and energized, inspired focus. Such an exceptional person and niece. Thank you!

- My broader family
    - Grandparents and my parents-in-law—you are gone but your impact on me is not forgotten, and yes, Gramma Lou, as you hoped, we definitely think of you now and again!
    - My nieces and nephews, aunts, uncles and cousins who all symbolize the importance of family relationships and I am so blessed to have come from such strong and close ones on all sides! It matters.
    - Everyone in the "Baker, Burrows, Stebbings" gang who represent the importance of extended family friend relationships.

- Our birth families—for the gift of our children and for the honesty, authenticity and courage to forge this unconventional and unprecedented kind of family relationship that is open adoption. We are truly blessed and richer for it. Our relationships confirm that there are never too many people to love your children!

- My "special people" who have had a significant impact on me and my life:
    - Barb—for over 25 years of walking and talking through the jolts. Gratitude for that reciprocal "holding the space" and the whole "you get me" piece.

- Jo—for the unconditional love and support for most of my life. For friendship at a deeper level than the word friend can adequately describe.
- Melinda, my coach, mentor, colleague and friend. For always being there—always holding me "big" so I could do the same for others, and for keeping me accountable to showing up at my best in all my roles.
- Lisa, my "go-to" support person for over 25 years— for your insight, patience, wisdom, challenges and unconditional belief in me. For helping me embrace, own and appreciate my complexity.

- My friends—I wish I could name you all, but you know you who are, and I can't begin to describe how significant you are and have been for me.

- My colleagues, teachers, professors and mentors who have impacted me deeply—even those who may not realize how profoundly.

- My clients—for the privilege of walking with you through your transitions—for your trust—for all that I have and continue to learn from you. It is an honour and a privilege!

- Nat, Stu and the Ultimate 48 Hour Author team—without your inspirational and effective process and support this book may have remained in my head forever instead of "out there". Thank you!

9 781922 597434